LONDON
NIGHT AND DAY

LONDON
NIGHT AND DAY

THE INSIDER'S GUIDE TO LONDON IN 24 HOURS

MATT BROWN

BATSFORD

First published in the United Kingdom in 2015 by
Batsford
1 Gower Street
London
WC1E 6HD

An imprint of Pavilion Books Group Ltd

Volume copyright © Batsford, 2015
Text copyright © Matt Brown, 2015
Illustrations by Andrew Joyce
Cover artwork by Martina Flor

ISBN: 9781849942942

A CIP catalogue record for this book is available from the
British Library.

20 19 18 17 16 15
10 9 8 7 6 5 4 3 2 1

Repro by Rival Colour Ltd, UK
Printed by Toppan Leefung Printing Limited, China

This book can be ordered direct from the publisher at the website:
www.pavilionbooks.com, or try your local bookshop.

To my nanna, Grace Brown (1925–2015), who once went
to London and refused free chocolate, on the grounds
that 'We're not from round here'.

CONTENTS

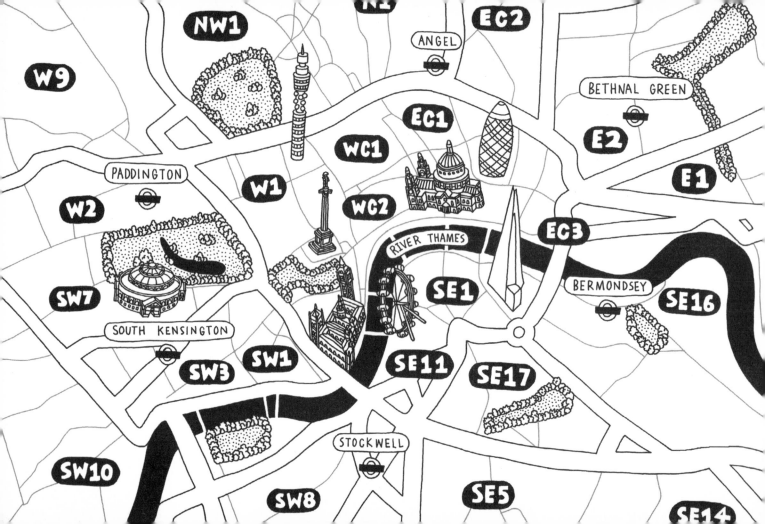

INTRODUCTION

In 1951, London played host to one of the greatest celebrations in the country's history. The Festival of Britain reinvigorated a tired, post-war city, spurred redevelopment of the industrial South Bank, and gave visitors a glimpse of a brighter future. Those visitors were not just Londoners. Hopeful pilgrims journeyed from all quarters of the UK, and from overseas. Like all visitors, they needed a guidebook to help them make the most of their time in London. Many were published; few had any longevity. And then there's *London, Night and Day* illustrated by Osbert Lancaster.

This remarkable guidebook raises eyebrows to this day. For cartoonist Lancaster and his anonymous scribe, the city was not some orderly metropolis to be catalogued and commended. It was a messy, dirty place with plenty of good and plenty of bad. Unlike many guidebooks of the day (and today), the book is filled with opinion and personal observation. Its other notable feature is that it follows the clock twice round, offering insights into the capital at every hour of day and night.

In September 2015, the inner workings of London are shifting gear once more. Five tube lines – the Central, Jubilee, Northern, Piccadilly and Victoria – will stay open all night on Fridays and Saturdays. The rest will follow a few years hence. This simple change to the transport network will have enormous repercussions for London. At a stroke, it will be much easier to move in and out of the city after midnight, both practically and – even more important – psychologically.

Although taxis and night buses have always made nocturnal socialising possible, the talismanic lure of the tube will undoubtedly swell the numbers willing to do so. This will inevitably result in a wave of new businesses such as all-night cafés and bars, and a revival of the clubbing scene, currently in the doldrums. Whole new mythologies and folk culture will undoubtedly emerge, as people get used to the horrors and the wonders of the 4am tube.

This seems, then, like the ideal moment to catalogue the 24-hour city as it currently stands (or otherwise). Drawing on Lancaster's 1951 volume for inspiration, this book is divided into 24 chapters, each following an hour of the clock, and what one might do within that hour. Of course, a book like this could never encapsulate everything that is possible in London, and simply to write a checklist of the very best would be lazy, when any competent Internet search will fulfil that need. Instead, like Lancaster's example, you will find me an idiosyncratic and occasionally opinionated guide. I'll reveal some of my favourite shops, restaurants and bars, but I'll also lead you along dark alleys, through industrial landscapes, and to parts of London you might never have heard of. The fruits of more than a decade exploring and writing about the capital are here caramelised into a collection of insights that I hope you won't find anywhere else. Above all, my aim is to instil a sense of wonder about what this great city offers, at any hour, day or night.

6 am

DAWN OF LONDON

Have you ever wondered where London came from? The start of the day is as good a time as any during which to contemplate the beginnings of the city.

Those of us who are still living in the capital in 2043 will surely hear all about it. That year will mark the 2,000th anniversary of the founding of the city, and the festivities will no doubt rival London's other great parties, such as the 1951 Festival of Britain and the 2012 Olympics and Paralympics.

Our city was established and named Londinium by a wave of conquering Romans around 43AD. No one is certain where the name came from, though it is likely to reflect an earlier Celtic origin. Before the Romans, there is no evidence of any sizeable settlement, but that's not to say nobody was here...

DISCOVER LONDON BEFORE LONDON

It's difficult now to imagine the land before the city, but there are places where the ancient landscape asserts itself still. Take a walk along King's Cross Road, for example, from Clerkenwell towards the terminus. See how the road meanders and twists? Notice how, after a while, the sideroads climb steeply away from you? You are walking along the valley of the River Fleet, and those gradients were cut from the clay many millennia ago. This primeval landscape has made its mark on the buildings as well as the street pattern. When you reach King's Cross station, seek out the new concourse. Its sweeping saucer shape is no accident. The roof was made this way to fit the curve of the neighbouring **Great Northern Hotel** (a good place to grab an early morning coffee, by the way). The hotel, in turn, has a curved profile because it follows the turn in the medieval Pancras Road. Why does the road bend at this point? Because it followed the banks of the River Fleet. The engineers who worked on the new concourse didn't know it (I asked them), but their building ultimately takes its modern form because of a river that existed before anyone had heard of stations, or railways, or London. (We might take things back one stage further, by observing that the river's course would have been determined at the end of the last ice age, when glacial meltwaters first carved out the Fleet Valley; and then to make the connection that the concourse resembles a giant glacier – but then we really are straying into the shadiest realms of psychogeography.)

You can find evidence of ancient rivers all over London. The Walbrook once flowed through the heart of Roman London. Its contours are still present in the valley between Ludgate and Cornhill, and a street named Walbrook follows its course. The Tyburn made its way through Marylebone and Mayfair before disgorging into the Thames at Westminster. A cursory glance at a street map readily reveals its meander – look for the twisty likes of Marylebone Lane and Bruton Lane, which stand out against the grid-like street patterns

of the West End. In south London, the Effra gave shape to Brockwell Park, runs round the boundary of the Oval and bequeathed its name to any number of roads, schools, pubs and cafés. Whole books have been written on the subject. Most of these rivers have long been culverted and turned into sewers – visible just at the Thames, where giant floodgates only release them in storm conditions. But they are still down there, waiting for a time when humans have abandoned London, and the ancient landscape can reassert itself.

There are other ancient sites around town, although time and tide have mostly erased the evidence. The Vauxhall and Nine Elms area is particularly noted for its prehistoric finds. A few years ago, timbers from 4,500BC were found in the riverside mud, just next to where the Effra meets the Thames. Whether this was a type of fishing pontoon or an early bridge is debated. You can only see the timbers during the lowest tides each year. Nearby, archaeologists working on the new US Embassy site discovered Paleolithic remains (as far back as 10,000BC) left by hunter-gatherers. It's not uncommon for flint tools of this era to be recovered from the Thames, though it requires a trained eye to interpret them.

Several locations in Greater London have ancient associations. Horsenden Hill near Sudbury Town tube

was home to an Iron Age community some 2,500 years ago. The view from the top is spectacular, all the more so considering that it has been appreciated since before the Roman conquest. This, in fact, is a great spot to watch the dawn, with the sun rising just to the side of Wembley Stadium. Meanwhile, a trip to Epping Forest (Theydon Bois tube) will reveal the remains of two Iron Age forts, hidden among the trees. Loughton Camp and Ambresbury Banks are both from around 500BC, retaining ditches and earthworks excavated 15 generations before Julius Caesar ever spied Britain. They are poorly signposted and require a bit of map-work, but this means you'll probably have them to yourself. There is no better spot in London to contemplate the ephemeral nature of life, and our tiny part in the turning of the centuries.

We can go still further back. As you walk around London, pay close attention to the stonework, especially on buildings made from white Portland stone. Many of these blocks contain tiny imperfections, with peculiar helical forms. These are the traces of ancient gastropods, bivalves and other small creatures that gave up their lives many millions of years ago. You can find these fossils on numerous buildings, including the Guildhall and the southern entrance to Green Park tube, which features particularly honeycombed stone. Strange to contemplate, but St Paul's Cathedral rests on the shells of a million ancient sea snails. You won't be told that by the tour guides.

SEEK OUT THE ROMANS

For its earliest years, London was engirdled and bounded by its old city walls. You can still trace their route around the Square Mile via a series of (rather dated) plaques. Outside Tower Hill tube station stands a tall section of surviving wall, presided over by a statue of Trajan, the emperor whose reign coincided with the first flourishing of Londinium as a major trading city. You can't follow the walls immediately north because of a new development, but head up Cooper's Row and into the courtyard of the Grange Hotel (it looks private, but there's a right of way). Here you will find London's most impressive section of wall. It towers over the courtyard and even incorporates an arch one can walk through. Much of the stonework is medieval, but if you look down into the pit you'll see the tell-tale red bricks of Roman origin.

The relics do not surface again until the revealingly named street known as London Wall. Fragments can be seen along this road, and are best glimpsed from the Barbican highwalk (where it still exists – another new development has dismantled part of it). The stretch towards the Museum of London is particularly bountiful, as we reach the part of Londinium that once contained a garrison fort. Remains of that structure can be seen along Noble Street and, on rare occasions of access, in the basement of the London Wall Car Park. The museum itself has a large Roman gallery (due for renewal soon), and an outlook on to a section of wall.

From here the wall headed south towards the Thames. No fragments remain above ground, but some pieces still exist in the basements of buildings along the route. The famous Old Bailey gets its name from the wall (a bailey is an enclosed courtyard), and indeed I've seen significant remains of the wall down in its basement, which are sadly not open to the public.

There are numerous other places to glimpse the legacy of the Roman Empire. Perhaps the most impressive ruins are to be found in the basement of the Guildhall Art Gallery (Bank), where stones from Londinium's amphitheatre were uncovered in the 1980s. This would have been a site of gladiatorial spectacle, and London's first sporting arena. The remains are eerily lit, and it's not unusual to find yourself completely alone down there.

Two churches, St Bride's on Fleet Street (Blackfriars) and All Hallow's-by-the-Tower (Tower Hill), also contain remnants of Roman structures in their crypts. The latter also houses a wonderful model of the Roman city, dating from the 1920s before the amphitheatre was discovered. Leadenhall Market, meanwhile, is built on the site of the old Roman Forum, the huge marketplace said to have been the largest structure north of the Alps. All that remains can be found in the small basement hairdressers on the corner of Gracechurch Street – book yourself an appointment and prepare to travel through time.

7 am

BREAKFAST

London has seen something of a breakfast Renaissance in recent years. Gone are the times when a greasy spoon fry-up or McChain hot muffin were the main options. Early morning dining is becoming something of an artform, no doubt given a fillip by the American and Australian obsessions with both breakfast and brunch. You can now break your fast with cuisines from all over the world. As with other food and drink sections in this book, space does not allow for anything approaching a comprehensive survey. Treat the following as a handpicked selection – some chosen for curiosity as much as quality – from the hundreds of excellent venues across town.

CENTRAL

Hamilton Hall
Liverpool Street Station, EC2M 7PY (Liverpool Street)

An increasing number of pubs now offer breakfast. The grandest and busiest of them all is this former hotel ballroom, long since converted into a mega-boozer by the Wetherspoon chain. The breakfast menu runs the full gamut of early morning favourites, from fry-ups to American-style pancakes. The real reason to visit, though, is to witness the troubling number of besuited executives necking a pint or two at 7am. No wonder we had a banking crisis. Most other Wetherspoon pubs in central London open for breakfast. I can also recommend the **Fox and Anchor** (115 Charterhouse Street, EC1M 6AA), which notionally caters for porters at Smithfield Market coming off shift, but is more likely to be filled with yet more office workers – a demographic catered for by the pub's 'City Boy Breakfast' option.

Regency Café
17–19 Regency Street, SW1P 4BY (Pimlico)

When it comes to the 'traditional café', plaudits usually go to the likes of **E Pellicci's** or **M Manze** (see page 17), but there are many other examples in less fashionable neighbourhoods.

The Regency is one such, occupying a quiet corner of Pimlico, and reasonably handy if you're visiting Tate Britain. The black tiles and frilly curtain give it an anachronistic film-set look from the outside (indeed, you might have seen it in the film *Layer Cake*). Within, you'll find a similar timewarp of Formica tables and photos of old football stars. This is a proper greasy spoon, where a stodgy Full English is the order of the day.

NORTH

The Breakfast Club
31 Camden Passage, N1 8EA (Angel)

The Breakfast Club, despite its name, offers top nosh at any time of day (and see 9pm for a rather special bar at the Spitalfields branch), but the queues often snake for a breakfast bite. Expect diner-style looks and a menu that mixes Full English, pancakes, oats and various egg creations – not all on the same plate. You even get a welcome from a cardboard Elvis, an ambassador for extraneous carbs if ever there was one. Other branches of this popular chain are popping up like toast across London, and now in Brighton.

Camino
3 Varnishers Yard, N1 9FD (King's Cross St Pancras)

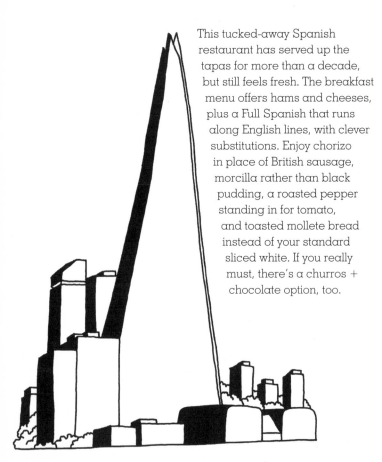

This tucked-away Spanish restaurant has served up the tapas for more than a decade, but still feels fresh. The breakfast menu offers hams and cheeses, plus a Full Spanish that runs along English lines, with clever substitutions. Enjoy chorizo in place of British sausage, morcilla rather than black pudding, a roasted pepper standing in for tomato, and toasted mollete bread instead of your standard sliced white. If you really must, there's a churros + chocolate option, too.

SOUTH

Aqua Shard
Level 31, The Shard, 31 St Thomas Street, SE1 9RY (London Bridge)

Start the day by overseeing the capital from this stylish panoramic restaurant in western Europe's tallest building. Aqua Shard has proved very popular, and evening reservations must be secured at least a month in advance. Not so breakfasts, which start from 7am and can usually be booked just a couple of days before. To its credit, the restaurant doesn't simply rely on its views to wow diners. All the usual morning classics are present and correct, but you can also sample a Lobster Benedict or sup a breakfast cocktail (one of which includes cornflakes).

Lido Café
Brockwell Lido, Dulwich Road, SE24 0PA (Herne Hill)

They say you should never swim on a full stomach. The temptation is certainly there at Brockwell Lido, which combines a gorgeous 1930s outdoor pool with one of the best cafés in the south. The caff offers the full range of usual suspects, with particularly good sourdough toasts and three degrees of Full English, to cater for different hunger levels.

EAST

Andina
1 Redchurch Street, E2 7DJ (Shoreditch High Street)

You could easily walk past this Peruvian kitchen, so very plain and understated is its façade. But this is London's trendiest street and, inside, all is vibrant – from the tightly packed tables to the swirling waiting staff. The food and drink is so colourful, you might want to bring sunglasses. Breakfast options (from 8am) include a Full Peruvian (fried eggs, pork rind known as chicharron, quinoa pancakes and more), and filo pastry with dulce de leche filling.

E Pellicci
332 Bethnal Green Road, E2 0AG (Bethnal Green)

Whole articles have been written about this traditional East End café. Queen Victoria was still on the throne when the Pellicci family, fresh from Tuscany, opened shop in 1900. It's still going strong with an interior untouched since the 1940s. Every Londoner passes this way sooner or later, from the Kray twins to A-list celebrities, to the legions of regular customers who live more humble lives. Serving from 7am, a huge Full English will cost you little more than a fiver, and in the most traditional setting you will ever witness.

WEST

Granger and Co.
175 Westbourne Grove, W11 2SB (Notting Hill Gate)

Aussie chef Bill Granger offers a taste of downunder, if that's not too unfortunate a mix of metaphors. First-timers should opt for the 'Full Aussie', an antipodean take on the traditional British breakfast, with added chipolatas and sourdough toast. You'll also find plenty of novel dishes, such as ricotta hotcakes (basically, American-style pancakes) with banana and honeycomb butter, or courgette fritters with deep-fried egg and halloumi. The whole ethos purports to be 'relaxed', but the place is always much too busy for that. A second branch can be found in Clerkenwell (50 Sekforde Street, EC1R 0HA).

Habanera
280 Uxbridge Road, W12 7JA (Shepherd's Bush Market)

There was a time when you couldn't find decent Mexican food in London for love nor money. Now you can chow down on Central American delights for any meal of the day. This colourful restaurant opens early on weekdays to dish out breakfast tacos and 'bacon & eggs burritos' to those who can stomach such things at the crack of dawn.

8 am

ESCAPING CENTRAL LONDON

It may seem contrarian, in these early chapters, to give instructions on how to leave the centre. I have a good reason, though. Outer London holds many of the most-interesting, best-kept secrets of the capital, but if you want to enjoy them it's best to make an early start. Plus, heading out of the centre just as all the morning commuters are trawling in gives one a sense of rebellion against the system. Every day should start with an act of non-conformity.

Barnet and surroundings
Barnet Museum, 31 Wood Street, EN5 4BE (High Barnet)

The northernmost point in Greater London is a small rhomboid of low deciduous woodland by the name of Tilekiln Osiers. I've never been, and wouldn't recommend that you go either, but it's always good to know these things. The outer limits of north London do hold many treasures, though. How about a visit to the ancient town of Barnet, at the top of the Northern Line? The area contains a number of attractive Tudor buildings and a landmark church. It was also the location of the Battle of Barnet (1471), a decisive confrontation during the War of the Roses. You can tour the battle site while climbing the hill up to the attractive village of Monken Hadley. Look back across the greensward for impressive views. Barnet Museum is also worth a visit, if only to see the portrait enigmatically labelled 'G. C. Hudson... hero of the Breeches Incident'. What can it all mean?

ENFIELD WAY

Forty Hall
Forty Hill, EN2 9HA (Turkey Street)

Whitewebbs Museum of Transport
Whitewebbs Road, EN2 9HW (Crews Hill)

Enfield, home of the eponymous rifle, is a sizeable area totally absent from most guidebooks. If you do make the journey, take a look around **Forty Hall**, a stunning Jacobean mansion surrounded by eminently explorable woods and fields. This former home of a Lord Mayor tells the story of life in the 17th century. Then, take the pleasant walk northwest to London's *other* transport museum, **Whitewebbs**. This small museum is so obscure it lacks a Wikipedia page and only opens Tuesdays and the last Sunday of the month. It's well worth a visit, though, for the collection of vintage cars, bikes, fire engines and other vehicles.

Queen Elizabeth's Hunting Lodge
8 Ranger's Road, E4 7QH (Chingford)

A little further to the east you'll find Epping Forest, a last tract of the Great North Forest that once covered most of the region. It's easy to get lost in the 6,000 acres (2,428ha) acres of beech and hornbeam, so begin by surveying the woods from Queen Elizabeth's

Hunting Lodge. This unique survivor from Tudor times served as a base and archery platform for royal hunting parties 450 years ago. It's now a mini-museum of Tudor life, perfect for family visits. From here, the still-vast forest stretches before you and would take days to explore fully. Be sure to carry a map, as mobile-phone signals aren't always easy to come by. There are many features to seek out, but the two Iron Age forts, mentioned in the opening chapter, are a priority.

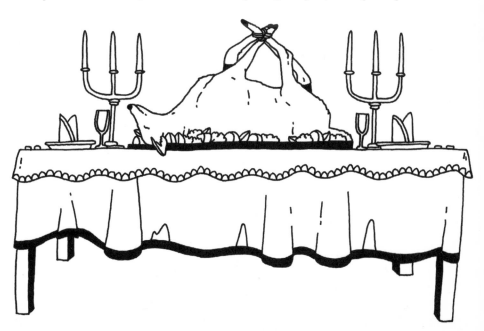

EAST

Barking and its Manors
Eastbury Manor House, Eastbury Square, IG11 9SN (Upney)
Valence House Museum
Becontree Avenue, RM8 3HT (Chadwell Heath)

Not many people go on a day trip to Barking, I'd wager, but it definitely has its charms. Any visit should include the remains of **Barking Abbey**, a major landowner in Medieval times. The town centre itself is surprising. Brightly coloured modern buildings (some perjoratively liken them to Lego) jostle with traditional brick builds and 1960s concrete. But the real star is **Eastbury Manor**, a 16th-century mansion house incongruously encircled by semi-detached housing. A tour takes a couple of hours, and includes impressive views from the turrets. Legend has it that the Gunpowder Plot was devised in this mansion. If you crave still more local history, take a 30-minute stroll to **Valence House Museum** in Dagenham. This attractive, timber-framed building serves as the borough's local museum, and very good it is too.

Rainham Marshes
New Tank Hill Road, RM19 1SZ (Purfleet)

At the furthest eastern reaches of London, stretching into Essex, lies Rainham Marshes, a supremely wild spot and one of the South-east's best destinations for birdwatching. A series of hides and reedbed boardwalks offer unrivalled vantage points to see swooping peregrines, whistling wigeons and flocks of lapwing. The marshland occupies former military land, and you can still find relics of the two World Wars lurking among the bulrushes. There's a nominal entrance fee, but the good people of the RSPB, who staff the visitor centre and café, will often waive it if you're a first-time visitor.

Upminster Windmill
The Mill Field, St Marys Lane, RM14 2QL (Upminster)

Even further to the east, but just within London's borders, stands the magnificent Upminster Windmill. This so-called smock mill has survived for over two centuries, and now opens to visitors on select weekends through summer (check the website for details). The nearest tube is Upminster, but you should take the slightly longer walk from Upminster Bridge to see that station's unusual concourse, which includes a large, tiled swastika, dating from a time when that symbol had no negative associations.

SOUTH

Chislehurst Caves
Caveside Close, Old Hill, BR7 5NL (Chislehurst)

Explore a London underground of a different ilk at Chislehurst Caves. These man-made caverns were hewn from the Kentish chalk untold centuries ago by Romans, or Druids, or Medieval miners. Despite what the guides might tell you, nobody really knows the origins of this 22-mile (35.4km) cave system, which only adds to the mystique. This Stygian realm became an underground city during the Second World War, as thousands of people sought shelter from the nightly bombing. That era is brought to life with a charmingly unconvincing series of mannequins. More costume can often be found above ground, where the local woods are used by live-action role-playing fans dressed as orcs, knights and wizards. There is undeniably a latent magic about this place.

Down House
Luxted Road, BR6 7JT (Orpington, then bus R8)

This quiet country retreat is not just a picturesque English Heritage house and garden, it was also home to Charles Darwin – one of the few human beings who will remain a household name for as long as there are households. For this reason, it has been nominated as a potential World Heritage Site, which would put it in the same category as the Houses of Parliament and the Tower of London. Because it is situated away from the centre in Bromley, it gets just a fraction of the visitors. The room in which *On the Origin of Species* was written will send a preternatural shiver down the spine of anyone who understands the immense importance of that work. For everyone else, well, just listen to David Attenborough's multimedia tour and you'll soon get your own spine tingles.

The White Cliffs of London
New Barn Lane, CR3 0EX (Kenley)

Did you know that London has its very own white cliffs? These chalky wonders can be found on the Neolithic site of Riddlesdown, towards the southern border of the London Borough of Croydon. Follow the London Loop walking path over this green space, until you ascend New Barn Lane. Look back, and there you'll see them... the White Cliffs of London. It's worth continuing along the London Loop for a few more miles. Eventually you'll reach Farthing Downs: this long strip of semi-wild greenery also rests on chalk, and commands epic views towards the City of London (which authority, incidentally, owns this land).

WEST

FOLLOW THE RIVER

The best way to explore west London is to follow the Thames. The riverside towns of Chiswick, Twickenham, Teddington, Richmond and Kingston all hold their charms. Chiswick gets its name from an old medieval cheese market or farm. This area was the country home of painter William Hogarth, but the Hogarth House Museum isn't as tranquil today, nestling as it does in the shadow of the Hogarth Roundabout. Nearby Chiswick House and Park are both worth a tour.

Twickenham's sporting attractions are world famous, but it's also a top choice for a riverside drink. **The White Swan** pub has one of London's most unusual beer gardens. At high tide, it becomes completely cut off from the pub. Ill-prepared drinkers can expect soggy socks. Teddington is home to famous television studios. The 'fish-slapping dance' from Monty Python was filmed on the lock here, which also marks the point where the Thames stops being tidal.

Richmond is a major town in its own right, with hundreds of shops, cafés, bars and restaurants. We'll visit the park in a later section, but for now, explore the postcard-perfect riverside. And note the old Georgian houses close to the bridge. These aren't 18th century at all, but modern pastiche designed by Prince Charles's favourite architect Quinlan Terry.

Kingston is another sizeable conurbation. It's often considered downmarket compared to Richmond, but this ignores an impressive history. Five Anglo-Saxon kings were crowned here, and you can still see the Coronation Stone in the centre of town. Kingston also contains one of London's oldest bridges, a short humpback affair known as the Clattern Bridge that spans the River Hogsmill.

FOLLOW THE CANAL

As well as the Thames, the west is also blessed with some of the capital's best stretches of canal. One very satisfying walk takes you along the banks of the River Brent, which meanders and merges with the Grand Union Canal. Start at Brentford Bridge, the scene of a small skirmish during the Civil War, and wind your way northwards through two centuries of industrial history. The canal is still used by industry today, as can be seen at the GlaxoSmithKline building, which takes in water to cool its colossal HQ. Further along, a couple of wooded spaces bring something more natural to the towpath. Towards Hanwell, I'd heartily recommend you break your walk with a quick (or long) stop off at **The Fox**, a homely, friendly local

with a staggering and award-winning choice of real ales. The waterway then bifurcates. Head west to see an impressive series of locks alongside an old asylum. These culminate in an astounding piece of Victorian engineering: a point where the canal passes over a railway and simultaneously tunnels underneath a road. This was Isambard Kingdom Brunel's last and least well-known major project, and is best viewed from the roadside above. More of Brunel's handiwork can be seen if you instead follow the River Brent at the branch point. This soon leads up into Hanwell proper, where you can see the **Braithwaite Viaduct** carrying the Great Western Railway over the Brent Valley. The nearby Viaduct pub commemorates the project, and offers views of the structure from its upstairs room (ignore the other windows, though, which face towards the concrete bulk of Ealing Hospital).

The Uxbridge area also gives good canal. This often-forgotten quarter is known to most Londoners only as the place that sounds a bit like Oxbridge and is situated at the end of the Metropolitan and Piccadilly Lines. The town centre is nothing special, but head a little further west for some of the most beautiful waterscapes in London. Here, the River Colne, River Frays and the Grand Union Canal perform an intricate dance around one another, occasionally inviting smaller watercourses into the quadrille while jealous lakes look on. The picturesque tangle coheres north of Uxbridge, at **Denham**

Deep Lock, where **Fran's Tea Garden** provides an idyllic stopping off point. Carry on north along the canal until you reach **The Coy Carp** – quite possibly London's most westerly pub – on the edge of Harefield. It's a homely place to finish up the perfect outer-London walk.

The hills of Northala
Kensington Road, UB5 (Northolt)

In 2008, London gained four new hills: this quartet of peaks is known as Northala Fields, and takes its name from the Old English version of Northolt, the nearest conurbation. The hills may lack vintage, but they pack in plenty of heritage. A million tons of rubble were transported from the demolition of the old Wembley Stadium, dumped beside the A40, and hewn into the verdant teats that stand here today. The largest peak offers excellent views across north London, and towards the crowning arch of the new Wembley.

AT THIS HOUR:

For those who can tolerate the frigid temperatures, an early-morning dip in one of Hampstead Heath's bathing ponds is a bracing way to start your day. The three pools, one for men, one for women and one mixed, open around 7am in the summer, or 8am in winter. It's £2 to get in.

9 am

SHOPPING

Let's get Oxford Street over in one sentence. There.
I'll also breeze past the leviathan Westfield shopping
centres at Shepherd's Bush and Stratford. The canny
London shopper avoids such noisy, crowded places in
favour of somewhere more individual. Those seeking
high-end fashions and designer clothing have picked
up the wrong book. I'm afraid I know next to nothing
about such vendors, other than that they tend to cluster
around Mayfair, St James's and certain chichi parts of
Marylebone and Knightsbridge. Besides, if you're after
a £20,000 Fabergé egg, you've probably got your own
personal shopper to assist you anyway. As elsewhere,
there are thousands of potential entries in this list, but
you're going to get my own idiosyncratic guide to some
of the capital's most memorable shops.

SOMETHING SHINY

London Silver Vaults
53–64 Chancery Lane, WC2A 1QS (Chancery Lane)

One pricey place that does deserve a peek is the London Silver
Vaults. This is the weirdest shopping mall you've ever been to.
It's buried a couple of storeys underground in old Victorian safe
deposit vaults, and contains 25 shops, nearly all dedicated to
silverware. You don't have to be any kind of expert, or even part
with any money to explore this lustrous labyrinth – just walk in,
have a look around, and chat to the friendly shopkeepers. It's
not all priceless Georgian tableware either: you can pick up
a small silver trinket, perhaps a christening spoon or napkin
holder, for as little as £20. A couple of the shops also trade in
vintage jewellery, offering something a bit different to nearby
Hatton Garden.

SOMETHING SWEET

Cybercandy
3 Garrick Street, WC2E 9BF (Leicester Square)

This place is your new best friend. If you're ever stuck for
a Secret Santa present, need a small, fun gift for a friend,

homesick expat, or just fancy an unusual treat, head along to this novelty sweet shop. Cybercandy stocks chocolate and candy from around the world. Want to try Japanese versions of British mainstays? You got it. Are you a fan of that hideous sick-flavoured chocolate that Americans seem to love? It's there. Want to know what custard-and-fish-finger chocolate tastes like? (hint: not all that impressive). You'll find it. Prices are a little higher than in regular shops, to cover import duties, but you can pick up a novelty treat for about £1. Branches can be found in Covent Garden and Angel.

SOMETHING FOODY

Persepolis
28–30 Peckham High Street, SE15 5DT (Peckham Rye)
A. Gold
42 Brushfield Street, E1 6AG (Liverpool Street)

Strolling down Peckham High Street it's impossible to miss the luminous yellow hues of **Persepolis**, a playful cornershop that specialises in Middle Eastern ingredients. It's equally impossible to miss the bright red shock of hair sported by the shop's proprietor Sally Butcher. The shop is annotated with delightful hand-written notes, to help newcomers get their heads around her stock. The tiny space occasionally doubles as an event venue, welcoming in punters for poetry nights or book readings. Sally's also written a handful of well-received cookery books, including a vegetarian guide to Middle Eastern cuisine. Meanwhile, **A. Gold** in Spitalfields is a delight for those seeking traditional British foods. Pick up a bottle of Henderson's Relish for the Northerner in your life; try a jar of honey made by King's Cross bees, or a tot of rum distilled in Walthamstow. They also dish out sandwiches at lunch, and irresistible Scotch eggs.

SOMETHING ARTY

Arty Globe
Unit 15, Greenwich Market, SE10 9HZ (Cutty Sark DLR)

The fun-sized Greenwich Market is always a joy to wander around, but the chief highlight has to be Arty Globe. This small shop to the southern end of the square showcases the handiwork of Hartwig Braun. His immediately recognisable designs all include colourful maps or panoramas of famous cities – London, more often than not. Prints of his hand-drawn creations are tempting enough, but you can also pick up scarves, jigsaws, T-shirts and other collectables that make for novel gifts.

SOMETHING BOOKISH

Copperfield's Books
37 Hartfield Road, SW19 3SG
(Wimbledon)
Skoob Books
Unit 66, Brunswick Shopping Centre, WC1N 1AE
(Russell Square)
Peter Harrington
100 Fulham Road, SW3 6HS
(South Kensington)
Oxfam
91 Marylebone High Street, W1U 4RB
(Baker Street)

Despite the rise of online alternatives and chain stores, the small, independent bookshop remains a cherished part of the London streetscape. The most fun can be had in second-hand shops, where you're always likely to stumble across long-out-of-print volumes that you never knew you needed. **Copperfield's Books** in Wimbledon is an absolute gem. Its shelves and tables are filled beyond capacity in a ramshackle, impossibly random jumble. Teetering piles of books hold up other teetering piles of books, to the point where you feel like you're playing a potentially bruising game of Jenga whenever you withdraw a volume. This is how all bookshops should be. The subterranean **Skoob** (that's 'books' backwards) in the Brunswick Centre is another favourite. This cavernous collection is bigger than it looks, and has a particularly fine section on London books. Charing Cross Road is the long-acknowledged place to go for antiquarian volumes, as immortalised in the delightful memoir/novel *84 Charing Cross Road*. Any of the surviving shops down there is worth a visit, as are the vendors of nearby Cecil Court, although prices can be off-putting for non-collectors. Those seeking first editions might try **Peter Harrington**, in Fulham and Mayfair. Although this, too, can be pricey, you can find some incredible stuff. I was once shown a first edition, author-annotated copy of Francis Grose's 1785 edition of his *Dictionary of the Vulgar Tongue*. I can now tell you the difference between a 'burning shame' and a 'flogging cully', though not in a family volume such as this. Finally, the best charity bookshop in London, for my money, is the nourishingly stocked **Oxfam** on Marylebone High Street. It might not be as decadent as the nearby **Daunt Books**, but its range is impressive, cheaper and helps a good cause with sales.

SOMETHING MAGICAL

International Magic Shop
89 Clerkenwell Road, EC1R 5BX (Farringdon)

London was a world centre of magic long before the *Harry Potter* novels. The Magic Circle, an organisation promoting the art of magic, was founded here in 1905, and still occupies a building near Euston. A more public venue has long commanded the corner of Clerkenwell Road and Leather Lane, in the guise of the International Magic Shop. It's been selling card tricks, hats from which to extract rabbits, wands and other appurtenances of the conjurer for half a century, with origins around the corner in the long-defunct Gamages department store. Wander in and learn how to levitate a cup or thrust a cigarette through a coin.

SOMETHING DESIGNER

Boxpark
2 Bethnal Green Road, E1 6GY (Shoreditch High Street)

One of London's unique shopping experiences can be had at Shoreditch's Boxpark. This miniature shopping mall has been constructed out of shipping containers, giving each business a narrow floorspace. The idea is to provide small, up-and-coming shops a chance to vend in a new location for lower rent. A few major brands like Nike have crept in of late, but the place still has an experimental feel. The lower row is mostly given to designer clothes and accessories, and it's a good place to pick up distinctive trainers, shades, headphones or handbags. Upstairs is the food deck, where you can find everything from Korean to posh fish and chips. Croydon is set to get its own Boxpark any time soon.

PUN SHOPPING

There was once a time when only hairdressers felt the need to enliven their trading names with a bit of wordplay: A Cut Above, A Snip at the Price, and North Finchley's double-punning Hair-O-Dyenamix might raise a chuckle. Nowadays, you can play a bountiful pun-hunting game on the high street. Eateries like Nincomsoup (Old Street), Fishcotheque (Waterloo) and Rock and Sole Plaice (Covent Garden) are perhaps the most numerous contingent, but look out, too, for the following ten shops:

Amazing Grates
fireplace specialists, 61–63 High Road, N2 8AB (East Finchley)

Floors For Thought
carpet shop, 103–105 Battersea Rise, SW11 1HW (Clapham Junction)

Frame Set & Match
picture framers, 41 Endell Street, WC2H 9BA (Covent Garden)

Frockney Rebel Vintage
vintage clothes shop, 49 Mowlem Street, E2 9HE (Cambridge Heath)

Get Stuffed
taxidermist, 105 Essex Road, N1 2SL (Essex Road)

Philglas & Swiggot
wine merchants, 64 Hill Rise, TW10 6UB (Richmond)

Planet of the Grapes
another wine merchants, 9 New Oxford Street, WC1A 1BA (Holborn)

R. Soles
shoe shop, 109A King's Road, SW3 4PA (Sloane Square)

Spex in the City

opticians, 1 Shorts Gardens, WC2H 9AT
(Covent Garden)

Turn 'em Clean

launderette, 11 Bedford Corner, W4 1LS
(Turnham Green)

Sadly, Stoke Newington's Sellfridges,
which sold fridges and was not to
be confused with the more famous
department store, has now closed down.

AND FINALLY…

Now long gone, the oddest shop I ever
encountered revelled under the name of
Shoot The Aged a 'Non-charitable, profit-
making shop' that stocked second-hand
furniture on the Lee-Blackheath borders.
It was last glimpsed around the turn of the
century, but has now disappeared without
trace. I can't imagine why.

10 am

LONDON AT WORK

Mid-morning and, at least on a weekday, much of the population are hard at work. You can join them, and have a bit of fun to boot, by visiting workplaces that offer public access.

CENTRAL

City of London Distillery
22 Bride Lane, EC4Y 8DT (Blackfriars)

An increasing contingent of spirit distilleries now operate in London. You can see how they work their alcoholic magic at a number of locations. The subterranean City of London Distillery puts on tours of its rather handsome stills and bottling facilities, as well as regular gin tastings. Likewise the **East London Liquor Company** which produces both gin and vodka at its home near Victoria Park.

Houses of Parliament
Do you really need the address? (Westminster)

It's also possible to watch our glorious leaders hard at work. Both the House of Commons and the House of Lords have public galleries, from which citizens and overseas visitors can watch the great debates of the age. You can usually turn up any weekday (except during recess), and simply join the queue at the Cromwell Green entrance, though be sure to bring photo ID. The exception is Prime Minister's Question Time, which is usually popular enough to be allocated by ticket (bizarrely, still acquired by writing to your MP). When Parliament is not sitting, public tours of the two chambers and the historic Westminster Hall are readily available.

London's Courts
Old Bailey, EC4M 7EH (St Paul's or City Thameslink)

Royal Courts of Justice
Strand, WC2A 2LL (Temple)

The judiciary at work can be scrutinised at two of London's most elegant buildings. More commonly called the Old Bailey, the Central Criminal Court has daily queues for its public galleries, with entry on a first-come, first-served basis. If you're lucky, you might catch a glimpse of the building's incredible frescoes in the main entrance lobby, and look out for the small shard of glass, still lodged in the ceiling, following an IRA bomb explosion in 1973. Similarly, one can readily visit the vast Gothic Revival pile that is the Royal Courts of Justice on the Strand, and wander into any court hearing. Be sure to take a look inside the main hall, a cathedral-like space with mesmerising floor tiling.

SOUTH

London Glassblowing
62–66 Bermondsey Street, SE1 3UD (London Bridge)

Peter Layton's studio on Bermondsey Street is a treat for the eyes. You can walk in whenever you like and watch the artisan glass blowers perfecting their skills. The studio's shop is filled with vitreous wonders, but you'll need to have broken through several glass ceilings in order to afford the larger items.

Blenheim Forge
Arch 229, Blenheim Court, SE15 4QL
(Peckham Rye Overground)

This modern-day smithy nestles in one of the area's many railway arches, where Jon Warshawsky and James Ross-Harris hand-craft superior knives for the capital's chefs and food obsessives. They even source wood for the handles from local parks. There's quite a waiting list for their products, but you can walk by anytime and peer into the forge.

EAST

Whitechapel Bell Foundry
32–34 Whitechapel Road, E1 1DY (Aldgate East)

This is reckoned to be the oldest manufacturer in the UK. Dating back to at least the 16th century, it has cast just about every famous bell in history: from Big Ben to the Liberty Bell

CHURCH BELL FOUNDRY

ESTABLISHED
A.D. 1570

(now in Philadelphia, USA), and many of the Square Mile's church bells. It's still going today, designing the clanger for the 2012 Olympic Games, and the Queen's Golden Jubilee bells. You can pop into the small foyer-cum-museum any time, but a full tour should be booked in advance (and there's a fair waiting list).

WEST

The Griffin Brewery
Chiswick Lane South, W4 2QB (Stamford Brook)

Of the dozens of brewers now fermenting in the capital (62 last time I counted in February 2015) around 15 offer behind-the-scenes tours, where you can learn about the craft of beer-making and try a few samples. The Griffin Brewery, on the banks of the Thames in Chiswick, has been around for centuries. It produces the ubiquitous London Pride, as well as many other well-known Fuller's tipples. £10 tours take place most weekdays. Smaller breweries elsewhere around town offer similar experiences and usually need to be pre-booked. Most are housed in industrial units, railway arches and other marginal spaces, producing beers with greater character and (often) strength than mainstream rivals. Personal favourites include **By The Horns Brewing Company** in Tooting, **Crate**

Brewery in Hackney Wick and **The Redchurch Brewery** in Bethnal Green, but you're guaranteed a friendly, tipsy time at any of them.

Darwin Centre
Natural History Museum, Cromwell Road, SW7 5BD
(South Kensington)

Of all the trades, that of scientist is perhaps the most inaccurately represented in films and media. Smoking, bubbling test tubes, mysteriously coloured lighting and eccentric hairstyles are absolutely not part of the mix – well, not usually – as you can see for yourself at the Natural History Museum's Darwin Centre. This distinctive, cocoon-shaped building offers visitors the chance to spectate as the museum's 220 research scientists go about their business, sorting beetles, sequencing DNA and tending to samples. You can even interrogate researchers about their work through a microphone connected to the laboratory.

AT THIS HOUR:

If you want to get into the opera or ballet on the cheap, join the queue for day tickets at the Royal Opera House. The venue holds back around 70 discounted seats every day for last-minute purchase at the Link Box Office (in the corridor that runs between Covent Garden and Bow Street). For popular productions (i.e. all of them), you'll want to get in the queue with plenty of time to spare. Only one ticket is allowed per person, unfortunately.

11 am

VISITOR ATTRACTIONS WORTH YOUR TIME

It's a common lament of the Londoner: 'I live among all these world-famous landmarks, but never visit any of them'. If that's you, then for shame. Many of the bigger attractions really are worth the entrance fee, and not just for holiday-makers. This chapter is as close as I'll get to the standard guidebook, but it's aimed more at Londoners who want to tick off the must-see sights of their home town.

CENTRAL

The Tower of London
EC3N 4AB (Tower Hill)

Perhaps the greatest example of 'I've never been' shame is the Tower of London. Yes, it's a major tourist magnet. Yes, you might have to queue. But once inside, you'll find a full day of distractions both entertaining and informative. The two chapels are particularly memorable. It's often forgotten or missed among the many other baubles here, but the White Tower contains London's oldest church, a Romanesque chapel dating from 1080. The Tower's other church, St Peter ad Vincula, is also of exceptional importance, though something of a johnny-come-lately at a mere 500 years old. It contains the graves of Anne Boleyn, Jane Grey, Thomas More and Thomas Cromwell, all of whom were executed nearby. Don't be shy of the Beefeater tours, either. Every yeoman warder, as they're properly called, has at least 22 years experience in the armed forces. They're proper characters and they know how to shout. I once had a pint (or three) with a former Beefeater; his booming voice and rambunctious temperament almost got us thrown out of the pub. And they also have to pass a rigorous history exam to lead the tours. Note: if you're a Tower Hamlets resident, you can get in for just £1.

HMS *Belfast*
The Queen's Walk, SE1 2JH (London Bridge)

Across the water, HMS *Belfast* is rewarding to explore. The numerous decks and cabins can be investigated at will, and it's refreshing to find a tourist attraction that lets you climb up and down ladders (don't wear a skirt) without safety-first supervision. The cruiser also holds the distinction of displaying London's most preposterous set of mannequins – with the possible exception of the Sherlock Holmes Museum. Odd fact: the ship's front turret guns are trained on the London Gateway service station at Scratchwood, some 11½ miles (18.5km) away.

National Gallery
Trafalgar Square, WC2N 5DN (Charing Cross)

London is blessed with a dozen major art galleries. The National Gallery will quickly become a firm friend once you've made the effort to visit. It contains absolutely no filler – every painting is a masterpiece. The crowds tend to hover around the Impressionist section, but I favour the back rooms with the sprawling 18th- and 19th-century canvases. Head along on a Wednesday morning and you can access the semi-secret 'Room A', a kind of glorified storage vault where the gallery keeps its 'also-rans'... any of which would sell for millions.

National Portrait Gallery
St Martin's Place, WC2H 0HE (Leicester Square)

The National Portrait Gallery is less grandiose, and less blessed with Old Masters than its conjoined twin, the National Gallery. It matters not, because its collection of famous faces – from Henry VIII to Dame Judy Dench – is endlessly engrossing. It's arranged chronologically from top to bottom, so head up the lanky escalator for the Tudor gallery, then work your way to ground level, which holds modern portraits. The gallery also boasts one of London's best museum cafés, with exceptional views over the rooftops around Trafalgar Square. A toast to Nelson is mandatory – especially if you encountered his portrait in the galleries below.

Museum of London
150 London Wall, EC2Y 5HN (St Paul's)
Museum of London Docklands
No. 1 Warehouse, West India Dock Road, E14 4AL (West India Quay DLR)

The Museum of London is one of those medium-sized museums that aims to satisfy both Londoners and visitors. As you'll readily guess, it tells the story of London from Palaeolithic times right up to the modern era. Highlights include the Lord Mayor's coach (unless he/she is using it), a recreated Victorian streetscape (go and sit in the pub and wait in vain for a pint), and the interior of a Victorian prison cell. The museum is at its best in the temporary exhibitions, which in recent years have covered populist topics such as Dickens and Sherlock Holmes with satisfying rigour. Sister venue, **Museum of London Docklands**, relates the history of the city's docks, from their role at the centre of the British Empire, to their near-utter destruction during the Blitz, and more recently their high-rise makeover. The museum is housed in one of the few buildings not to be razed by the firestorm of the 1940s.

Tate Modern
Bankside, SE1 9TG (Blackfriars or Southwark)

This is one of the world's newest major galleries, opening in 1999 in a former power station (designed, incidentally, by the same architect who gave us the red phone box). Its reputation, and its proximity to St Paul's Cathedral, make this a tourist mecca, but every Londoner should also make its acquaintance. Even if modern art leaves you cold, the building is a joy to wander around just for its architecture. The enormous Turbine Hall has enough space for everyone, and houses commissioned works that could not fit in any other gallery. A new extension, looking something like a crooked pyramid, is due to open in a year or so, if they ever get round to laying the brickwork.

Tate Britain
Millbank, SW1P 4RG (Pimlico)

Sister gallery Tate Britain can be found a mile or so upriver, in Millbank, and regular boats connect the two. This venue displays (mostly) British art from Tudor times to the modern day and is particularly prized for its Turner collection. Again, the building's architecture is a huge part of the experience. The entrance lobby, Duveen Gallery and undercroft are among the most striking spaces in London. A recent rehang has greatly improved orientation, but sapped the life out of the labelling.

British Museum
Great Russell Street, WC1B 3DG
(Holborn, Russell Square or Tottenham Court Road)

Finally, the British Museum. Avoid this place at all costs during high summer and Christmas time. The museum is right up there on the tourist itinerary with Buckingham Palace and Tower Bridge and gets extremely busy during peak times. Instead, make your pilgrimage in spring or autumn, preferably early in the morning, to appreciate the collections at their most serene – not to mention the breathtaking glass ceiling of the Great Court. The revamped Anglo-Saxon galleries are vital, and contain the unprecedented treasures of the Sutton Hoo excavation. The Japan galleries on the top floor, and the African galleries in the basement are both superbly laid-out, and seem to be less popular with the crowds. Finally, the enormous Enlightenment Gallery contains boundless cabinets of curiosity, displayed in a traditional manner. It's not always open but try to get a peek inside the old Reading Room, formerly the British Library, where the likes of Karl Marx and George Orwell spent many an afternoon.

WEST

Victoria and Albert Museum
Cromwell Road, SW7 2RL (South Kensington)
Natural History Museum
Cromwell Road, SW7 5BD (South Kensington)
Science Museum
Exhibition Road, SW7 2DD (South Kensington)

This eminent trio of museums are all world-class. Every Londoner should make it a mission to get to know them. You have to be careful with your visiting hours, however, as they all get tremendously busy. Here are a few tips, gained from long experience.

Natural History Museum Be sure to use the side door (Exhibition Road) to avoid the queues. Beware of the dinosaurs – here be dragons, plus thousands of children. The Earth Galleries are usually less crowded, and offer more adult material than many of the other spaces. Seek out the great blue whale model (surprisingly well hidden considering its size) and ask the attendants about the time capsule supposedly buried inside. Finally, climb the stairs to the top of the older building to enjoy the stupendous architecture, including dozens of animal forms carved into the superstructure.

Science Museum A favourite with school groups, this place gets busy both in and out of term time. Unlike the NHM, however, it's cannily (if not officially) divided between areas for kids and places for grown-ups. The recently built Communications gallery is a must (you may remember the Queen declaring it open with her first Tweet). Here you'll find the earliest TV, and the computer upon which the World Wide Web was first developed. The Flight gallery is also fun and, practically concealed at the back of an upper floor, is always peaceful. The whole museum is best visited on one of the monthly late openings (usually the last Wednesday of the month), when it's adults only … even in the 'hands-on' area usually aimed at children. You can drink wine, too.

Victoria and Albert Museum The largest of all London's museums and the only one that contains, in Orwellian fashion, a 'Room 101'. The V&A is a sprawling collection of all that is good in design, from fashions to architecture. Because of its size, and lesser appeal to youngsters, this museum tends to feel less crowded than its brethren. My favourite section is the sumptuous Medieval and Renaissance galleries – a collection so vast it took me ten visits to view everything. The recently revamped Casts Courts are unmissable: this is the world's greatest collection of plaster-cast facsimiles of famous sculpture, from Michelangelo's *David* to Trajan's Column. Don't miss, either, the famous Cartoons by Raphael.

Hampton Court Palace
East Molesey, KT8 9AU (Hampton Court)

If the Tower of London gave you a taste for royal refuges, you should also seek out Henry VIII's great pile at Hampton Court Palace. It celebrates its 500th birthday in 2015, which makes it only about half the age of the Tower, but its rambling Tudor buildings and parkland setting give it a greater sense of grandeur. Plus, you get two palaces for the price of one, with William and Mary's baroque addition grafted on to the old Gothic buildings. The Stuarts wanted to knock Henry's palace down and build a rival to Versailles. Fortunately for us, they ran out of money before much of the Tudor structure

AT THIS HOUR:

Of all the London experiences deemed 'only for tourists', going to watch the Changing of the Guard must rank highest. But everyone should experience it at least once. It takes place from 11.30am every day (every other day in winter). First, pick a day when the Queen is at home – you can tell this by the Royal Standard flying over Buckingham Palace. The ceremony includes bonus soldiers whenever the sovereign is nearby. To see the full changeover, you need to get to the Palace at least 30 minutes before the start to bag a good spot at the railings. If you're not bothered about the ceremony itself and just want to see 30 or 40 marching soldiers, hang out on Birdcage Walk (St James's Park tube) around 11.15am, and you should have a close-up view of the new guard marching to the Palace.

was lost. I once had the pleasure of a trip onto the roof, whose access stairs still contain smoke damage from the disastrous fire in 1986. With its unrivaled history, endless gardens, spooky reputation and superb programme of events including a winter ice rink, I judge Hampton Court Palace as the best all-round attraction in the capital – both for tourists and Londoners.

EAST

MARITIME GREENWICH

National Maritime Museum
Park Row, SE10 9NF (Cutty Sark DLR)
Cutty Sark
King William Walk, SE10 9HT (Cutty Sark DLR)
Royal Observatory Greenwich
Blackheath Avenue, SE10 8XJ (Cutty Sark DLR)
Old Royal Naval College
King William Walk, SE10 9NN (Cutty Sark DLR)

Greenwich, or more properly Maritime Greenwich, is designated as a World Heritage Site. Of all the tourist sites listed in this section, it has the most to offer for Londoners, and rewards a repeat visit. **The National Maritime Museum** is the largest museum of ships and the sea in the world. Check out its new(-ish) Nelson exhibition, and the beautiful stained glass rescued from the bombed-out Baltic Exchange in the Square Mile. The museum also looks after the *Cutty Sark* clipper ship. Following a disastrous fire in 2007, the 19th-century vessel has been fully restored. The surrounding glass canopy is something of a love/hate structure from the outside – it looks as though someone has built an approximation of the sea in Minecraft – but it all makes sense from below decks. Up on the hill, meanwhile, you'll find the **Royal Observatory Greenwich**. The tourists keep themselves busy bestraddling the famous Greenwich Meridian Line, but there's plenty to see indoors in the observatory's astronomy galleries. It also contains London's only planetarium. Don't neglect the classic buildings either. Christopher Wren's **Old Royal Naval College** is to some people as much of a masterpiece as his cathedral at St Paul's. And be sure to take a look around the Painted Hall, London's answer to the Sistine Chapel. The nearby **Queen's Gallery** offers a final flourish of culture, with dozens of canvases on a nautical theme.

12 noon

LUNCH

Fans of queuing wait till 1pm, but those with sense in their heads grab lunch at midday. It's a banality to write that London has an almost infinite choice of places to eat. And long gone are the days when a sandwich was your only lunchtime option. Anyone who invested in salmon farms or edamame plantations must surely be a millionaire by now, given the rapid growth of the sushi and salad sectors.

Meanwhile, hot food is also on the rise as a lunchtime option: countless soup shops, chickenmeisters, Thai kitchens and rebooted Italian takeaways now do a roaring trade. The biggest trend of all has seen parades of street-food vans clustering into market areas, selling everything from gourmet burgers to artisan cupcakes.

A final trend has seen a rise in novelty gimmick eateries. In the past couple of years, Londoners have enjoyed two cat cafés, a rat café, a cereal café and one offering brunch for dogs. At the time of writing, there's talk of an owl bar in Soho, where diners share their tables with birds of prey. Such places might raise a smile, but they also tend towards the ephemeral, so are not listed here.

CENTRAL

Whitecross Street Food Market
Whitecross Street, EC1Y (Old Street)

Whitecross Street is among the largest and best established of the street-food markets. Every weekday, 30–40 stalls open up to serve hot food to the hungry workers. You really have to get here at noon unless you're prepared to queue. Vendors tend to stick around, with everything on offer from venison burgers (Wild Game Co.) to burritos (Luardos). The early time slot will also bag you a table in The Two Brewers pub, mid-way along the street, which lets market customers take their food inside as long as they buy a drink. The Barbican's lakeside terrace is also a short walk away, and always has free tables.

Scandinavian Kitchen
61 Great Titchfield Street, W1W 7PP (Oxford Street)

Is it a shop? Is it a deli? Is it a café? No, it's all three. This permanently trendy Scandi outlet can get a little crowded, but that's all part of the fun. Our north European brethren know how to do breads and cheeses, and the rye bread is especially delish.

Nincomsoup
7–8 St Agnes Well, EC1Y 1BE (Old Street)

St Agnes Well is the official name for that slightly awkward set of cafés and shops beneath the Old Street roundabout. Businesses come and go here, but Nincomsoup has been trading for years – a pioneer in the resurgent soup scene, and the best named by far. It serves up six different concoctions every day, with veggie, meat, fish and exotic options.

Café in the Crypt
St Martin-in-the-Fields, Trafalgar Square, WC2N 4JJ (Charing Cross)

A number of London churches have found a new source of income by converting their crypts into dining rooms or cafés. Even St Paul's Cathedral is in on the act. Such spaces are always atmospheric and convivial, so long as your appetite is not troubled by the proximity to human remains. St Martin-in-the-Fields is the best of the lot, with its illuminated groin vaults and tombstone paving. I once read the whole of *Dracula* down here. The food is canteen-style with reasonable (for the West End) prices. Appetite sated, you can head into an adjoining room and try your hand at brass rubbing.

NORTH

Gallipoli
102 Upper Street, N1 1QP (Angel)

I don't have this as a confirmed fact, but I'd wager that Upper Street in Islington contains more restaurants than any other road in London. They change hands faster than anyone can keep track of, but this lovely Turkish café-restaurant has been around as long as I can remember. It can get very busy of an evening (a popularity that has now spawned two spin-off venues), so lunch is perhaps the best time to see it. I'd recommend the liver wrap for those who would, or the halloumi version for veggies.

MADE Bar and Kitchen
Roundhouse, Chalk Farm Road, NW1 8EH (Chalk Farm)

The Roundhouse's much-loved restaurant-bar is a classy but relaxed affair – it was no surprise to be seated at a table beside newsreader Jon Snow on one visit. Because it's attached to one of London's premier live performance spaces, things can get busy in the evening, pre-show. So slink by for a spot of lunch and enjoy the space at its quietest. The all-day fare is modern British, but I'd recommend the 'Quick lunch' options, which are a steal at £6.50. In the summer, head upstairs to visit the popular 'Camden Beach', a sand-topped roof with a cocktail bar.

SOUTH

M. Manze
87 Tower Bridge Road, SE1 4TW (Borough)

If you're looking for a traditional Cockney lunch, then anything with Manze in the name is a good bet. At least five of these family caffs still enrich the streets of London. The Borough version is the oldest, and still looks the part with Edwardian tiling and original recipes. If I might be allowed a moment of mild iconoclasm, the traditional pie, mash and parsley liquor might be a little bland to the modern palate, but the experience – both authentic and charming – more than makes up for this. It's cheap, too.

Brixton Market
Atlantic Road, SW9 (Brixton)

The various covered walkways and colourful streets that make up Brixton Market are gaining a reputation to match even Borough Market. The eastern-most section, known as Brixton Village, seems to win the most plaudits with foodies

Fridays are also your chance to catch a free classical concert. The London Symphony Orchestra plays inside the atmospheric old church of St Luke's (Old Street) most weeks at 12.30pm. You can't book – just turn up and walk in for a lunchtime musical treat.

for its bewildering collection of small cafés and restaurants. I've seen people queuing *in the snow* for a seat at homely Thai café Kaosarn. Franco Manca's sourdough pizzas on nearby Market Row proved so popular that the business has since expanded into an impressive chain, with 12 London restaurants and counting. I could go on, but the real joy of the market is to wander round and follow your whims.

EAST

Japanika
10 Hanbury Street, E1 6QR (Shoreditch High Street)

Most of the big sushi chains will serve up decent offerings these days, but you're still better off going to the independents. One of my favourites is Japanika, right next door to Poppie's Fish and Chips in Spitalfields (see page 95). The £7.99 variety box is the benchmark by which I judge all other sushi shops.

The Gallery Café
21 Old Ford Road, E2 9PL (Bethnal Green)

It's impossible not to fall in love with this homely-yet-bustling café. The green paintjob on the outside reflects the eco-friendly, sustainable business running on the inside, where all dishes are vegetarian or vegan and universally delicious. Lunch is the most relaxing time to visit, but pop by in the evening for live events, including quizzes and music. All profits are put back into the parent charity St Margaret's House, as a final right-on touch.

WEST

The Alice House
53–55 Salusbury Road, NW6 6NJ (Queen's Park)

I like the Alice House – obviously, or I wouldn't be recommending it. In theory, it's much like any other smart, modern bar-restaurant, with exposed brickwork and matching wooden tables. And yet it's somehow more laid-back, lacking any pretension and serving as something of a community hub. You'd feel equally welcome with just a coffee, a full three-course meal or a pint of craft ale. The lunch menu offers various iterations of stuff-on-toast, well presented and well priced. A sister venue in West Hampstead does much the same thing, though suffers from too much popularity.

Electric Diner
191 Portobello Road, W11 2ED (Ladbroke Grove)

An American-style diner next to one of Britain's oldest cinemas, the Electric is a long-time favourite of locals and those living further afield. Its welcoming booths and gently barrelled roof provide a cosy setting in which to enjoy US classics such as ribs, burgers, hot dogs and the currently ubiquitous pulled pork.

AT THIS HOUR:

Have you ever seen a bridge curl up into a ball? Head to Paddington Basin (Paddington) on Fridays at noon to see this remarkable feat of pontine dexterity. The Rolling Bridge spans a short water channel on the northern side of the basin. Once a week, someone presses a button, and it curls back in upon itself like some kind of steel caterpillar. It was designed by Thomas Heatherwick who is now more famous for the Olympic Cauldron, New Routemaster and Garden Bridge.

1 pm

PARKLIFE

London is said to be one of the greenest capitals in the world. This immediately becomes apparent if you go a few floors up. From the rooftops, even awful thoroughfares like Kingsway and Euston Road appear as verdant strips, with great London plane trees densely packed. But it is to the parks that we turn for a true taste of *rus in urbe* (or 'country in the city' for those not versed in Latin).

CENTRAL

The Royal Parks
St James's Park (St James's Park)
Green Park (Green Park)
Hyde Park (Marble Arch, Lancaster Gate or Hyde Park Corner)
Kensington Gardens (Queensway)

The central Royal Parks are the most famous, and the most popular among tourists. Stately **St James's Park** boasts the best groundsmanship, with numerous flower beds and an ornamental lake, where you can watch the park's colony of pelicans attempt to swallow the pigeons (it really has been known). Neighbouring **Green Park** lacks any flower beds, hence its name. An old legend relates that Charles II's queen caught the Merry Monarch parading with a mistress in the park. In a fit of pique, she ordered that all the flowers be plucked, and thus it remains to this day. The floral absence focuses more attention on the towering trees throughout the park. Look, too, for the sloping valley, carved out by the River Tyburn, now buried underground as a sewer.

The third park in the chain comprises **Hyde Park** and **Kensington Gardens**, which stretch for a mile or so to the west of centre. The former is best suited for lounging or playing ball games, while a hardy bunch of swimmers take to the Serpentine lake in all weathers, most famously during the Christmas Day swim. Kensington Gardens, meanwhile, is more sedate, as you'd expect for the gardens surrounding Kensington Palace. This park contains many notable monuments including the Peter Pan statue and the Albert Memorial. Best of all, though, is the Elfin Oak to the north-west. This 900-year-old tree stump, originally from Richmond Park, is carved with dozens of elves and gnomes – a delight for children.

City of London pocket parks
Christ Church Greyfriars Newgate Street (St Paul's)
Postman's Park St Martin's Le-Grand (St Paul's)
St Dunstan-in-the-East St Dunstan's Hill (Monument)

Often overlooked, the City of London contains dozens of tiny 'pocket parks'. These green spaces are the former burial grounds of the medieval city's churches, now converted into picturesque spots in which to chew your sarnies. Others have been crafted from the churches themselves. **Christ Church Greyfriars**, designed by Christopher Wren, is a striking case in point. Its tower still stands following a careful reassembly, and is now a private residence. The bombed-out nave, however, has been beautifully transfigured into a vibrant rose garden. Nearby, you'll find **Postman's Park**: this small space,

by inviolable law, must always be included in books on 'quirky London'. It is well known for its memorial to humble people who gave their lives saving others. Best of all is **St Dunstan-in-the-East**. Its Christopher Wren spire looks just like Thunderbird 3 from the old puppet show. It presides over another shattered nave that now contains a bubbling fountain, creeping ivy and plenty of benches. There is no spot more tranquil in the whole of London.

SOUTH

Greenwich Park and beyond
(Cutty Sark DLR)

Once seen, never forgotten. The steep slope up to the Royal Observatory affords supreme views of the curving Thames and the multiplying skyscrapers of Canary Wharf. To the east of the park, you'll find many elevated but quiet corners where tourists fear to tread – the perfect place to picnic in the summer. The park also contains Roman remains and a little-known deer sanctuary to the south. Head beyond the walls here, and you'll find yourself on the plain of Blackheath, whose preternatural aura is partly ruined by the heavy lines of traffic passing through. It's a bit of a trek, but if you're feeling adventurous, head up Shooter's Hill to find the bizarre

OBSCURE GEM

Regent Square
(King's Cross St Pancras)

Don't confuse Regent Square garden with Regent's Park. It's about 10,000 times smaller. It includes, however, several oddities I suspect few people are aware of. Look up in the trees to see an aviary of plastic birds. Meanwhile, the lawn contains an utterly pointless bollard, placed there as part of some situationist art project. Note also the ancient 'ghost sign', still advertising medicines to 'cure all wounds and sores' on the south side of the square.

Severndroog Castle, whose recently reopened roof provides sweeping views of the south-east. The surrounding Oxleas Wood is also very lovely, and very ancient, with an unbroken lineage of trees stretching back to the end of the last Ice Age.

Crystal Palace Park
(Crystal Palace)

Further south is the mighty Crystal Palace Park. This historic open space is famed for its collection of dinosaur models (I don't think anyone's ever realised it, but only a few of them are actually dinosaurs … most represent extinct mammals or fish… but they're always referred to as dinosaurs). The most striking feature is an absence. The great Crystal Palace burned down in 1936, but its footprint can still be found to the south of the park.

Wimbledon Common
(Wimbledon)

The Common, Wimbledon Park and neighbouring Putney Heath would take a lifetime to explore adequately: 1,137 acres (460ha) of woodlands, scrub, fields and lakes cover an area similar to a medium-sized town. It's impossible to wander round without whistling the theme tune to the classic '70s TV show, *The Wombles*, but I'd instead direct you to Michael de

Larrabeiti's deliciously anarchic novel *The Borrible Trilogy*, which sees a tribe of mischievous child-things hiking to the Common in order to murder a warren of thinly disguised Wombles. Features of interest include the famous windmill, a Grade II*-listed structure with a small museum. Towards the common's midriff is a quaint hamlet containing a handful of houses and a top-notch gastropub, the Fox and Grapes. Nearby Cannizaro Park provides yet more outdoor space to explore. This is certainly a good part of town in which to own a dog, or a pair of running shoes.

Burgess Park
(Elephant and Castle)

Perhaps less well known, at least to non-locals, is Burgess Park, just south of Old Kent Road. The park was built after the Second World War, reclaiming a heavily blitzed area of housing. This recently re-landscaped green space contains an impressive artificial lake, which was supposedly lined with the world's largest sheet of waterproof plastic when it was originally created. The southern end of the park includes a walkway that follows the route of the long-filled-in Surrey Canal. Redundant bridges still arch over the path, and other pieces of canal infrastructure are everywhere. Much of the canal's route has been transformed into a linear park, which stretches all the way down to Peckham.

EAST

Victoria Park
(Cambridge Heath or Hackney Wick)

Two great parks can be found to the east. Victoria Park is the oldest, boasting plenty of open space, a recently restored Japanese garden and particularly beautiful stretch of canal

OBSCURE GEM

Stave Hill
(Canada Water)

Stave Hill in Rotherhithe is woefully under-appreciated. This artificial mound was created from the rubble of nearby dock buildings, demolished following the decline of the city's river trade. Hidden away in dense woodland, it's a surprise to reach the summit and behold the views of Canary Wharf.

where I swear I've seen terrapins paddling about. Look out for the two stone niches with seating inside at the eastern end. These are remnants of Old London Bridge, moved to the park in the 1860s.

Queen Elizabeth Olympic Park
(Hackney Wick or Stratford)

Further east is London's newest major green space: the Queen Elizabeth Olympic Park. It's the only park to be opened twice: once for the Olympics and Paralympics in 2012, and then again a year later, following re-landscaping. As a recent creation, it lacks mature trees and can feel a little windswept. In summer, though, a meander beside the network of rivers and wildflower meadows is very relaxing. I hear that otters have been spotted here, too.

WEST

Richmond Park
(Richmond and North Sheen)

Not to be outdone, West London contains the magnificent Richmond Park. In places, this can feel a little wild and windswept, especially when you catch sight of the roaming

OBSCURE GEM

Central Park
(East Ham)

Did you know London has its own Central Park? It's situated off the High Street in East Ham. The park contains some unusual sculptures of what appear to be lottery balls embedded in rock. These sit next to a couple of Victorian iron columns whose provenance is unknown (at least to me, to Google and the local tour guide I asked).

deer. Head to the western end and you'll find a very different scene, and one that might seem familiar: the view along the Thames to Windsor is among the most-painted scenes in Britain. While you're over there, ascend King Henry's Mound to see a view of a different calibre. A narrow tunnel has been cut through the foliage, allowing an uninterrupted and protected sightline to St Paul's Cathedral, some 10 miles (16km) away.

OBSCURE GEM

Acton Park
(Acton Central)

Look high in the branches of Acton Park: one of the London plane trees contains a model of a python. I have no idea why. Perhaps it's a visual pun on the movie *Snakes on a Plane* (tree).

Bushy Park
(Hampton Wick)

Across the water, the vast Bushy Park is less well known, but a joy to explore. It must be London's wildest park, and the Royal Park with the fewest visitors. You can find yourself in pockets of silent isolation, punctuated only by the shrill cry of the ring-necked parakeet, a species that now completely dominates the area. Keep an eye out too for the free-roaming deer that tend to loiter to the north-east.

NORTH

The Regent's Park and Primrose Hill
(Regent's Park or Chalk Farm)

The final Royal Park in our roll call is The Regent's Park. Perhaps the most varied of London's green lungs, this large open space is known for its elegant flower gardens, football pitches, boating lake and, of course, ZSL London Zoo. A pleasant hour can be spent walking north through the park and on towards Primrose Hill, from where you'll get one of the best views of the capital.

Hampstead Heath
(Hampstead)

A couple of miles north is the magnificent Hampstead Heath, a mix of woodlands, open spaces and **Kenwood House** – a swish art gallery set in a stately home. One of the Heath's greatest assets, and not as well known, is the pergola complex over to the west. This Italian-style, raised promenade wends its way through the trees, before arriving at a viewing point looking towards Harrow. It is the most romantic walk in London, especially with the wisteria in bloom, and it is usually quite deserted.

OBSCURE GEM

Antrim Gardens
(Belsize Park)

This tiny garden, backing on to an allotment, is not much of a space, but it does contain two curious relics: a balustrade from the old Waterloo Bridge, and a fragment from the blitzed House of Commons. Many locals don't know these antiques are here.

2 pm

SMALLER ATTRACTIONS

London contains well over 100 small museums, countless galleries, and an ever-changing selection of pop-up displays and exhibitions. Space does not allow any kind of comprehensive survey, so I've included the absolute must-sees, and a few personal favourites. Once you've been to a couple, visiting these smaller museums becomes addictive. They're often much quieter than major venues, too.

CENTRAL

The central areas of town conceal countless small galleries and cultural centres, far too numerous to list out in full. For starters, the streets around Cork Street in Mayfair are bejewelled with dozens of small commercial galleries, while Soho and Fitzrovia are no slouches either.

LINCOLN'S INN FIELDS MUSEUMS

Sir John Soane's Museum
13 Lincoln's Inn Fields WC2A 3BP (Holborn)

Hunterian Museum
The Royal College of Surgeons, 35-43 Lincoln's Inn Fields, WC2A 3PE (Holborn)

Most guidebooks rave about the **Sir John Soane's Museum** in Lincoln's Inn Fields, fêteing it as a 'hidden gem' and 'off the beaten track'. It is neither of these things, just a two-minute walk from Holborn tube station, and situated in London's largest square. However, the house museum is still worth a visit to see its unique displays of posh bric-a-brac: busts, balustrades, urns, paintings and pediments are all cluttered together in a kaleidoscope of antiquities. Even more startling, on the other side of the square, is the **Hunterian Museum**. This comprises the London collection of the Royal College of Surgeons, and contains many a grizzly exhibit – from diseased tissues to a giant's skeleton. Kids will love it; parents will cower.

The Foundling Museum
40 Brunswick Square, WC1N 1AZ
(Russell Square)

From the Hunterian, it's not too far to walk to the Foundling Museum in Bloomsbury. This small venue tells the story of Thomas Coram's remarkable home for abandoned children, which occupied this site until well into the 20th century. That tale is interesting enough, but the Foundling Hospital also had impressive sponsors, including Handel and Hogarth. Both are represented in the museum's permanent displays, and there's a rolling programme of temporary exhibitions. Good café, too. Once you're done, be sure to head through the brutalist Brunswick Centre to Marchmont Street, where you'll find a trail of foundling tokens (mementos left by mothers, alongside their babies so they might one day reclaim them) embedded in the pavement.

New London Architecture
The Building Centre, 26 Store Street, WC1E 7BT
(Goodge Street)

One small museum-cum-gallery that deserves to be much better known is the somewhat awkwardly named New London Architecture just off Tottenham Court Road. This is a useful place to visit if you're fairly new to town. Why? Because the centrepiece is an enormous three-dimensional map of London, recently updated so that it now stretches from Earl's Court in the west to the Royal Docks in the east. Other than commandeering a helicopter, there's no better way to get a feel for the geography of London, as well as learning more about upcoming plans for new buildings in the capital. (There's also an hilarious tradition of placing unlikely figurines such as dinosaurs and giant robots on the map – I presume it's students from nearby UCL.)

Gagosian Gallery

6–24 Britannia Street, WC1X 9JD (King's Cross St Pancras)

This wealthy space looks like it's going to be tiny, but opens up inside to show off big-name temporary exhibitions. The place was packed to the gunwales with Picassos a few years ago, for example.

WEST

West London is not always appreciated as a cultural centre. This is to do it a disservice, for the region is particularly good for local museums. Sadly, both the Gunnersbury Park Museum (Hounslow) and Pitzhanger Manor House and Gallery (Ealing) are closed for major renovation, and will not

be open until 2016 and 2018 respectively. Both may safely be added to this list thereafter.

Museum of Brands, Packaging and Advertising

2 Colville Mews, W11 2AR (Notting Hill Gate or Ladbroke Grove)

Notting Hill is home to what, on the face of it, sounds like an unpromising offering. The Museum of Brands is, however, a delight for nostalgists. It displays decades' worth of packages from thousands of familiar products. You'll come out whistling the song from the Ovaltine or Kia-Ora adverts, depending on your age.

Boston Manor House

Boston Manor Road, TW8 9JX (Boston Manor or Brentford)

A manor house has stood on this site for the best part of 1,000 years, but the current house-museum is from the 17th century. This former Jacobite mansion contains a series of period rooms, and a unique staircase. Look out for the painted angel above the fireplace in the Drawing Room; she bears a striking (if coincidental) likeness to Margaret Thatcher. The stately gardens slope down to the River Brent, where you can pick up the river walk mentioned in the 8am chapter (page 23).

Leighton House Museum
12 Holland Park Road, W14 8LZ (High Street Kensington)

Perhaps more of a gallery than museum, this house was formerly the home of Lord Leighton, one of the 19th century's most famous British painters. Many of his canvases and sculptures can be found here, but it is the unforgettable Middle Eastern fantasy of the Arab Hall that will stay with you the longest – all mosaics and Islamic tile designs. Its every crevice is embellished with some noble ornament, gilt carving or intricate tile pattern.

Gloucester Road Tube Station
(Gloucester Road, obviously)

Not a lot of people know this, but Gloucester Road is the capital's most-visited gallery, with some 14 million entries and exits each year. Most of these visitors are, of course, catching trains, but while they do so, they might care to glance at the station's row of blind arches on the disused platform. Since the turn of the Millennium these have served as niches for striking pieces of art. Installations along this wall have included a 7m (23ft) high panda's head, a pile of mattresses, English landscapes and a giant A-Z.

SOUTH

The south is as culturally rich as any other quarter, and perhaps more diversely so, with everything from a fan museum (Greenwich) to a museum of sewing machines (Tooting Bec). Sadly, one of the south's true cultural gems, the Cuming Museum at Walworth, was badly damaged by fire in 2013. If it ever reopens, consider it worthy of a place in the following list of some of the area's stronger attractions.

Old Operating Theatre and Herb Garret
9a St Thomas Street, SE1 9RY (London Bridge)

This remarkable museum can be found at the top of a church tower in London Bridge. The space was used as a training theatre for surgeons at nearby Guy's Hospital, but was then boarded up and only rediscovered a few decades ago. The museum is particularly geared up for family visits, if you can get nervous little ones past the grinning skull above the museum entrance.

Surrey Docks City Farm
Rotherhithe Street, SE16 5ET (Surrey Quays)

London contains many city farms, including notable examples at Spitalfields, Kentish Town, Vauxhall and Mudchute on the

Isle of Dogs. My favourite is Surrey Quays Farm. It is sited just off the Thames path opposite Canary Wharf and seems to spill out on to the riverside (via plaques and displays, not escapee animals). Inside, kids of all ages can enjoy mingling with pigs, goats, cattle and other beasts. Mummy and daddy, meanwhile, can enjoy a quiet cuppa in the friendly café.

Horniman Museum
100 London Road, SE23 3PQ (Forest Hill Overground)

It seems somewhat inadequate to include the Horniman Museum in a section of smaller museums and galleries. This wonderful institution is fairly large and contains much-loved collections on natural history, musical instruments and ethnic costume. The museum's mascot is a malproportioned walrus, poorly stuffed in the Victorian age but still holding his ground in the natural-history section. The sundial trail in the gardens is a heap of fun, and offers surprising views of London from this hilly location.

Bold Tendencies
Levels 7–10, Peckham Multi-storey Car Park, 95a Rye Lane, SE15 4TG (Peckham Rye) Note: summer months only.

South London's oddest art gallery can be found occupying the top floors of an old multi-storey car park. The route to the top

is haphazardly signposted, and can feel a little intimidating if you're not entirely confident that you're in the right place. Persevere, though, and you'll gain an experience you'll never forget. Sculptural art, of varying quality, is strewn across the decks. The rooftop commands spectacular views looking north to central London, and includes a popular Campari bar called Frank's, which can become exceptionally busy on warm summer nights.

EAST

The east is, these days, a world-famous centre of art and fashion, with dozens of galleries clustering in Shoreditch, Hackney, Bow and particularly the canal-side enclave of Vyner Street (although there are signs that this may be on the wane). For every permanent gallery, there's probably another three or four temporary 'pop-ups' colonising abandoned shops and other properties. Last year, for example, one artist took over an old corner shop and stocked it entirely with hand-made felt versions of popular foodstuffs. The First Thursdays initiative is a good way to explore this bewildering scene. As the name suggests, it takes place on the first Thursday of every month, when galleries across east London open late, often with refreshments. Otherwise, here are a few excellent places to start, including a few small museums.

Dennis Severs' House
18 Folgate Street, E1 6BX (Liverpool Street)

The spirit of the old East London is most successfully evoked at Dennis Severs' House in Spitalfields. This old silk-weaver's home is a time capsule, re-creating bygone days in decor and drama. The series of rooms, all in different styles, was slowly pieced together in the 1980s by the eponymous Severs, a Californian who settled in Spitalfields when the place was depressed and run-down. Following his death in 1999, the home became a living memorial both to the man, and to the domestic history that so fascinated him. The performance-led tours are best experienced by winter candlelight.

Sutton House
2–4 Homerton High Street, E9 6JQ (Hackney Central or Homerton)

This red-brick manor house is reckoned to be the oldest residential building in the borough of Hackney, dating back to Tudor times. It's now managed by the National Trust, and gives visitors a glimpse into the home life of wealthy 16th century Londoners. In a peculiar juxtaposition, you'll also get a taste of a 1980s squat: during that decade, the house had fallen into disrepair, and was used as a kind of impromptu community centre. A graffitied wall has been retained.

The Geffrye Museum
136 Kingsland Road, E2 8EA (Hoxton)

The Geffrye Museum runs from a series of quaint Grade I-listed almshouses next to Hoxton station. It tells the story of home interiors through the centuries via a sequence of chronological rooms. The effect is particularly charming during the Christmas season, when each room is given period decoration. The museum is about to undertake a major new development that will create 40 per cent more space, including a new café in a formerly derelict pub (saved from demolition after much public lobbying).

STREET ART GALLERIES

Howard Griffin Gallery
189 Shoreditch High Street, E1 6HU (Shoreditch High Street)
Pure Evil Gallery
108 Leonard Street, EC2A 4XS (Old Street)

The east is also well known for its street art scene, and several small galleries have sprung up to turn this once-edgy artform into something potentially quite lucrative. The **Howard Griffin Gallery** is one such example, set up by the eponymous owner after his passion for running street art tours spilled over into mounting exhibitions. The Pure Evil gallery nearby, meanwhile, is curated by the artist of that name, whose vampiric animals are still a common sight around London.

NORTH

North London is often stereotyped as the land of left-wing, Guardian-reading bookish types. Playing up to that image, my selection of recommended cultural centres is of a somewhat intellectual bent.

Freud Museum
20 Maresfield Gardens, NW3 5SX (Finchley Road)

This house museum presents the history of the great psychoanalyst in his former home, including his extensive collection of antiquities, which might be considered as a miniature rival to the John Soane's Museum. Here you'll also find Freud's study and the famous psychoanalytic couch, one of the most iconic items of furniture in the world (and off-world, for a replica even appeared in *Star Trek: The Next Generation*). Look out for the seated statue of Freud, one of the finest bronzes in London, a little down the hill on Fitzjohn's Avenue. Meanwhile, nearby Camden Arts Centre (Arkwright Road, NW3 6DG) has an ever-changing range of contemporary art and a rather nice garden-café to enjoy.

The Jewish Museum
129–131 Albert Street, NW1 7NB (Camden Town)

This Camden Town venue tells the history of Judaism in Britain, alongside displays on ceremonial art and the Holocaust. Housed in an anonymous-looking Victorian terraced house, the museum sparkles on the inside, following a refit at the start of the decade.

Zabludowicz Collection
176 Prince of Wales Road, NW5 3PT
(Chalk Farm or Kentish Town West)

About a mile away from the Jewish Museum, the Zabludowicz Collection nestles behind a weighty Corinthian portico – a former Methodist chapel – so wonderfully alien to both the surrounding terraces and the often-challenging contemporary art inside. It's worth a visit for the architecture, even if the exhibitions don't suit your tastes. It has sister galleries in New York and, unusually, on a Finnish island.

William Morris Gallery
Lloyd Park House, 531 Forest Road, E17 4PP
(Walthamstow Central)

Morris is one of those rare Londoners whose life spawned more than one museum or gallery. Indeed, I'm pretty sure he has more London cultural centres than any other subject, with further properties in Bexleyheath (east), Merton (south) and Hammersmith (west). The northern compass point of Walthamstow boasts his family home for eight years, now converted into a museum of his life, designs and collaborators. Walthamstow in general now enjoys a thriving arts scene, with numerous galleries dotted throughout the area. Look out for the annual Walthamstow Arts Trail, when these small spaces are linked together and supplemented by pop-up galleries in pubs and halls.

AT THIS HOUR:

St James's Park has been home to a colony of pelicans since the 17th century. The big-beaked birds get a late lunch every day at 2.30pm. Simply pop along to the eastern end of the park and watch as they're dealt a fish supper.

3 pm
GLORIOUS MINUTIAE

Mid-afternoon is a good time to amble through the streets, taking in the details one might normally miss. The city seems a little quieter, caught in a lull before school runs and rush hour.

Here are three short walks pointing out some lesser-known oddities in well-known areas. You'll need some kind of map, digital or otherwise, to help navigate.

"GIRO"

EIN TREUEN BE GLEITER

LONDON IM FEBRUAR 1934

HOESCH

WESTMINSTER

Start at **Admiralty Arch**. There's a nose on the inside of one of its portals. No, seriously. Look just above head height on the north-west side, and there it is. Popular myth declares it the symbolic nose of the Duke of Wellington, and that all soldiers must rub it as they pass through. It's all nonsense. The nose is one of dozens appended to the walls of London over the years, a project initiated by artist Rick Butler. Only about ten remain, including the one on the Arch. A particular concentration can be found in Soho, and one enterprising guide offers occasional tours.

Now, we're going to find central London's most secret alleyway. I know a few Westminster tour guides who've never heard about it. Head up Spring Gardens then, as you reach the British Council building, carry on straight ahead beneath the arch. Aim for the tall conifer. To its left you'll find a narrow passage and steps – it even has its own bit of sculpture at the top – leading to Carlton House Terrace. Walk along this extremely posh street, noting the various institutions and statuary. You should have no problem finding the Grand Old Duke of York. The nursery-rhyme soldier perches on top of a large column, regularly mistaken for Nelson, halfway along the street. This granite erection was used for London's first outdoor demonstration of electric lighting, in 1848. Right next to the Duke of York's column you will see a large plane tree. Beneath, and unseen by most passers-by, is what appears to be a miniature garden shed. Still curiouser, a German memorial stone inside commemorates **Giro**. This was the dog of German Ambassador Leopold von Hoesch who presided over the nearby Embassy just before the Second World War. The pooch was buried with full Third Reich honours and is often referred to as 'Giro the Nazi dog', but in truth, the hound's political leanings were never recorded. A little further along Carlton House Terrace is the site of that Embassy, now the **Royal Society**. This august scientific body, which holds regular free events for the public, recently celebrated its 350th anniversary. If you can't get in for a snoop around its marbled halls, at least observe the door handles, which contain sculptures representing the DNA double helix.

The German influence on the street continues towards its end, where you'll find various plaques and a statue to Charles de Gaulle. The big-nosed General set up the headquarters of the Free French here after being driven out of France by the Nazis following the invasion in 1940. His statue was unveiled by the Queen Mother in 1993. As you descend on to the Mall from Carlton House Terrace, you'll find a rather lovely memorial to her as well, including some superb panels in high relief showing scenes from her life.

Head back north along the Mall, and turn right just before Admiralty Arch onto Horse Guards Road. Note the imposing and windowless concrete building on the corner. This is a rather obvious military bunker known as the **Admiralty Citadel** and described by Winston Churchill as a 'Vast monstrosity which weighs upon the Horse Guards Parade'. The vines draped over the top help. A bit. The **National Police Memorial** in front of it conceals a ventilation shaft for the tube.

Continue on to **Horse Guards** itself. This ancient parade ground has been used by Royal troops since at least Tudor times, and you'll see a couple standing guard as you pass through the arch (ignore the tourist farrago). Once out on Whitehall, cross the road and look back at the clock tower of Horse Guards. See the black mark at 2pm? That signifies the hour at which King Charles I was beheaded in 1649, pretty much on the spot where you're standing outside the **Banqueting House** (pay the fee and head inside if you want to see an incredible Rubens ceiling).

Let's look at one last oddity round here. Head north along Whitehall until you come to the Silver Cross pub on the right-hand side. Craig's Court, the short street leading off to its side, is thought to contain an entrance to a complex of secret tunnels. Known as Q-Whitehall, this set of passages connects up the various government buildings in the area, allowing bigwigs to wander back and forth without having to encounter the hoi polloi.

BANKSIDE

Start outside **Shakespeare's Globe**, the modern re-creation of the Bard's great theatre. What most people don't realise is that it was rebuilt (deliberately) in the wrong place. We'll see the original location in a short while. For now, have a quick look around the Globe's courtyard, which includes a number of notable features. The wrought-iron gates almost hide in plain sight, but are among the most important modern sculptures in London. They depict over 100 plants, creatures and objects from Shakespeare's plays, and were crafted by blacksmiths from all over the country. The courtyard itself is paved with stones acknowledging donor names. John Cleese paid for two, one for himself and one for Michael Palin. In typical Cleese style, he insisted that his fellow Python's name should be misspelled, and thus Michael Pallin is immortalised.

Leave the court and cast your eyes west, where a row of quaint 17th-century houses gives a flavour of old Bankside. One of these dwellings, marked with a plaque, was supposedly occupied by Sir Christopher Wren while he oversaw the building of St Paul's Cathedral on the other bank. The other peculiarity is the narrow and fenced off **Cardinal Cap Alley** running between two of these buildings. It was possible, until land disputes in the 1990s, to walk along the alley. I have it on good authority that it also served as a popular resort for illicit nocturnal encounters when the area was not so bustling as it is today.

Head east along the river and duck along **Bear Gardens**. This short street gets its name from the bear-baiting ring that once stood here. The sport was so popular that a swollen crowd caused the stands to collapse in 1583, killing eight spectators.

At the end of the street turn left on to Park Street. Head along until you've passed under Southwark Bridge and you'll immediately see a large plaque to the right. *This* is the site of the **original Globe theatre**, marked out in coloured tiles across the paved area. It's tantalising to ponder what archaeological remains might exist beneath the nearby row of houses.

Carrying on along Park Street, the housing estate beyond the next corner was once home to the **Anchor Brewery**, one of London's major manufacturers of beer. It was established in 1616, the very year of Shakespeare's death, and eventually demolished in 1981. The Anchor pub nearby is the only physical reminder, but a series of plaques gives some history of the site. My favourite, round on the northern continuation of

Park Street, commemorates the 'international incident' when a bunch of brewery draymen handed out a sound thrashing to a noted brute called General Haynau, otherwise known as the 'Austrian Butcher'. I can't think of any other plaque that celebrates a mugging.

From here, all roads lead to **Borough Market**. But look out for the scruffy old properties beyond the railway bridge, next to the Little Dorrit café. These have become simulacra of 'rough and ready London' in any number of films, most notably *Lock, Stock and Two Smoking Barrels* (1998). While you're here, see if you can find the entrance to the Leaky Cauldron from the *Harry Potter* films (clue, it's round the corner), and the flat belonging to Bridget Jones.

HOLBORN

Local business groups have been trying to rebrand this area as Midtown for years – an eminently sensible, and therefore utterly inappropriate candidate for a London place name. We must call it Holborn, and we must pronounce it properly; that is, using as few letters as possible. Aim for 'O'b'n', rather than 'Hole-bourne'. (That said, the latter is closer to its original derivation, meaning a hollow near the river, or borne.) We'll start with the British Museum tourists, piling out of

Holborn tube station to confront one of the worst crossroads in the capital. Turn right and head east along High Holborn, just a short way before turning right again into **New Turnstile**. The curious name relates to times of yore when Holborn was used to drive cattle up to Smithfield Market – the turnstiles were pedestrian routes that would not allow livestock. Turn left at the end, and follow this passage to its conclusion. Here you can see **Lincoln's Inn Fields**, the largest square in London, to your right and another alley to the left. Take the alley. No good reason, other than that the passageways of London are worth learning as valuable shortcuts and sidesteps around crowded pavements. You'll pass **The Ship**, one of the oldest pubs in the area, and a former gathering place for the Catholic faithful during the centuries of persecution and mistrust.

Back out on Holborn, cross the busy road and head forward to **Red Lion Square**. This small patch of green is supposedly haunted by the shade of Oliver Cromwell, whose exhumed corpse was stowed overnight in a nearby pub, on its way to be ceremonially hanged by Royalists. Less ridiculous is the nearby **Conway Hall**, a centre of rationalist and humanist debate for decades. It runs a nourishing events programme, and it's always worth sticking your head in to see what's happening.

It's hard to escape pubs and ghosts in this part of town, and we're approaching one of the capital's most curious pairings. **The Dolphin** at the end of Red Lion Passage was struck by a Zeppelin bomb in the First World War. Several people were killed. A clock, damaged beyond repair in the raid, still hangs in the tiny tap room, frozen at the time of impact. Its hands never move, but it's said to chime the hour on the anniversary of the attack. Head north now, along **Lamb's Conduit Street** (the neighbouring Lacon House is a former government building whose name is an abridgement of the street). This is one of London's most traditional shopping streets, with artisan bakers, specialist book shops, pricey wine bars and exclusive fashion boutiques… plus the wonderful Sid's Café, with its ever-reliable jacket potatoes. Long may such contrasts blossom beside one another, for this is the true character of London.

Great Ormond Street leads you past the famous hospital into **Queen Square**. George III convalesced here during his famous madness, and The Queen's Larder pub recalls his spouse's local accommodation. There's a statue of Queen Charlotte in the square, although some say it's Queen Anne. The same Zeppelin raid that did for The Dolphin's clock also struck this square, but without consequence. The eagle-eyed will find a plaque marking the exact spot in the middle of the lawn.

4 pm

A RELAXING CUPPA

It used to be said of London that you're never more than a few feet away from a rat. The same truism might now be applied to the coffee shop. They're everywhere, both chain and independent shops. Prices vary wildly. A cappuccino can still be procured for under £1 in certain 'greasy spoons' and Italian-style delis, although the quality is likely to be low. At the upper end, richly brewed bevvies occasionally exceed the £4 mark, especially if you're drinking in. You'll notice the quality, and the hole in your purse. The average price, at least among chain coffee shops, seems to have settled somewhere around the £2.20 mark for takeaway.

But where to go? If you're prepared to pay for quality, then you're most likely to find it in an independent shop. For some reason, these often sport one-word names like 'Nude', 'Dose', 'Kaffeine' and 'Workshop'.

Another trend employs the use of cheery phrases, like 'Tina We Salute You' and the cycling-obsessed café 'Look Mum No Hands'. All share a passion for proper coffee, usually made from locally roasted beans. I like to play a little game of ordering a cappuccino in the afternoon, just to see if any of the baristas get sniffy about this social faux pas. Never happens, though, for indie coffee shops are universally staffed with polite, charming people.

True coffee fiends would argue the merits of individual beans, bars and baristas, but most people, including myself, don't have palates that could rank these nuances. The following, then, is my own personal selection, which is influenced more on how much I like sitting in these places than any acts of arcane beanmanship.

Oh, and Soho's Bar Italia would undoubtedly make my list, but I'm saving that for 2am.

CENTRAL

Half Cup
100–102 Judd Street, WC1H 9NT (King's Cross St Pancras)

My current favourite is this relatively new coffee shop. It's only a short walk from St Pancras, but just far enough away to escape the hordes. For similar reasons, it has a relaxing rather than trendy vibe, and much more seating space than the typical independent. Love it. The nearby **Moreish** café (76 Marchmont Street, WC1N 1AG) is also a worthy stop, with more of a food offering, and excellent window seats from which to watch pedestrians attempt to cross London's most ludicrous cycle lane.

The Attendant
Downstairs, 27a Foley Street, W1W 6DY
(Goodge Street or Oxford Circus)

If you think modern coffee prices are taking the piss, here's one venue that revels in the allusion. The Attendant is a subterranean café housed inside a Victorian men's public toilet. I'd walked past the elegant ironmongery many times over the years, wishing that the long-closed convenience might be recalled to life. My wish came true, in a most peculiar way, in 2013. You can now tuck your legs into a porcelain urinal, whose curvaceous partitions make for surprisingly elegant table dividers. Really, it has to be seen to be believed. There's nothing crappy about the food and drink, all scrupulously sourced from ethical suppliers, and the best sandwiches you'll find in any lavatory, anywhere.

Cabbie's shelter
Embankment Place, WC2 (Embankment)

This distinctive green hut near the Playhouse Theatre is one of 13 remaining cab shelters dotted around town. It's still used by cab drivers and the public are not permitted inside. You can, however, order a very cheap cup of tea from the takeaway serving hatch on the side. Hardly darjeeling at the Ritz, but an amiable experiences that is unique to London.

NORTH

Gran Sasso
44–46 Caledonian Road, N1 9DT (King's Cross St Pancras)

I have to admit that the contrarian in me has chosen this one. The no-frills traditional Italian coffee shop has none of the twee trappings of the more trendy independents (such as Drink, Shop, Do just across the road … I'm looking at you).

Instead, you can expect a genuinely warm welcome from Val and Mario, attentive service and prices about half the rate elsewhere (again… cf. Drink, Shop, Do).

The Legal Café
81 Haverstock Hill, NW3 4SL (Chalk Farm)

With a name seemingly implying that all other cafés in the area are somehow illegal, this curiosity on the slopes of Hampstead is a must-visit for all seekers of oddness. The conundrum is resolved once inside. It turns out that the café is attached to a law firm, and you can order a legal consultation alongside your skinny latte. It's not, of course, mandatory, and I'd much rather spend money on a barista than a barrister.

Yumchaa
The Granary Building, N1C 4AA (King's Cross St Pancras)

The trend for ever-more-sophisticated coffee shops has left the humble cup of tea somewhat abandoned. Yumchaa is on a mission to revive the beverage, with a number of branches across the capital. This one recently opened just inside the main campus building of Central St Martin's, and it's a doozy. No tea bags here. Instead, you choose from a bewildering set of loose-leaf options, arrayed in sniffable containers on the counter. If the weather's fine, you can take your brew of choice outside and watch the dancing fountains of Granary Square. Civilised has a new definition.

SOUTH

Láng
The Shard, 32 London Bridge Street, SE1 9SG (London Bridge)

Western Europe's tallest building contains many bars and restaurants, all of which are inevitably more spendy than eateries with less altitude. You can, however, grab a top-grade coffee for £4 in this ground floor café, part of the Shard's Shangri-La hotel. The only view is of people heading up the escalators, but you can enjoy impeccable service and a mightily tempting range of cakes, and then tell your friends you dined in the Shard.

No. 67
67 Peckham Road, SE5 8HU (Peckham Rye)

Cafés don't come more homely than this independent business betwixt Camberwell and Peckham. Indeed, it's built into an old home – complete with front and rear gardens – tacked on the side of the South London Gallery. The place stays open all day and evening, turning into a bar-restaurant later on, but I reckon a mid-afternoon cuppa is the best time to catch it.

EAST

The Bridge
15 Kingsland Road, E2 8AE (Hoxton)

This Hoxton mainstay has to be seen to be believed. The downstairs makes an artform out of clutter, with antique boxing gloves, costume hats and a stray viola all vying for wall space. The upstairs is equally eccentric, resembling an over-furnished Victorian brothel. They do offer takeaway coffee, but with this decor, leaving would be an outrage.

Hoxton Hotel
81 Great Eastern Street, EC2A 3HU (Old Street)
199–206 High Holborn, WC1V 7BD (Holborn)

Hotels are an often-overlooked option for coffee. Many are pricey or perhaps seem too formal for a casual stop-off. Not so Shoreditch's Hoxton Hotel, which is abuzz all day with business meetings and friendly catch-ups. A coffee costs £3–4, which isn't bad given the stylish surroundings and friendly table service. The formula has been so successful that a sister hotel has now opened in Holborn. The hotel's fortunes are curiously mirrored by the **Grind** mini-chain of coffee shops, whose first branch was also in Shoreditch (213 Old Street, EC1V 9NR), and second is next door to Hoxton Hotel Holborn.

Giddy Up
Various locations across town

We all have one of those friends who has a knack of appearing randomly in the most unlikely places. The peripatetic Giddy Up is a bit like that. We've encountered their little one-man stalls in obscure parks, city streets and even outside the Guildhall. You could find out where they're currently trading from their website or Twitter, but I always believe that they'll find you, in the very moment when your need for caffeine is greatest. Not only do they serve superior artisan coffees, they also help out young ex-offenders by training them up in hospitality skills. Coffee with a conscience.

WEST

Paperback Coffee & Tea
153 South Ealing Road, W5 4QP (South Ealing)

I had no business being in South Ealing. I think I only got the train there because I'd heard it was one of only two tube stations to contain all the vowels. But I've since revisited twice purely to spend an hour in this smashing little coffee shop. The vibe is relaxed, yet playfully undermined by witty notes on coffee-shop etiquette (this is not a place to bring bawling children). Coffee is locally roasted; the tea selection is huge and exotic. In a nod to the shop's name, you can leave or take paperback books from the shelves dotted around. The last time I visited there was a bit of a sci-fi thing going on.

Bubbleology
45 Pembridge Road, W11 3HG (Notting Hill Gate)

I've only ever tried bubble tea twice. I'm not sure it's for me, but the Taiwanese tea with chewy tapioca balls certainly has its adherents. You only have to visit this branch of the mini-chain Bubbleology for evidence. I've yet to walk past without seeing a queue out of the door -- especially in summer when Notting Hill fills with tourists. When you finally get to the counter, the range is boggling with available flavours such as taro, papaya and kumquat.

CHAINS

Coffee chains are usually less expensive, with the trade-off being that you get weaker drinks and less individuality. Nevertheless, their brews are generally very drinkable, if nothing remarkable. It's easy and fashionable to bash coffee chains, but they sometimes offer advantages you wouldn't find elsewhere. So, to the horror of coffee snobs everywhere, I'm going to finish by recommending the very best of the maligned mainstream.

Starbucks: The branch in Liverpool Street Station is decked out like a Georgian dining room with beautiful wooden panelling quite unlike anything else inside the station. The café in St Katharine Docks, meanwhile, inhabits a rotunda building known as The Coronarium. This was formerly an all-faiths chapel and is surely the only Starbucks whose building was originally opened by the Queen. Finally, the Camden Town branch sits charmingly along the canalside and maintains a somewhat unexpected small museum of Camden history inside.

Caffè Nero: If you look carefully, you'll find a branch inside the horseshoe of Broadcasting House. I say 'look carefully' because it's the only Nero that doesn't have its distinctive blue-and-black logo emblazoned above the door. This is because it's positioned directly opposite the glass-walled studio in which *The One Show* is filmed. The BBC's rules disallow any form of product placement, hence no nameplate.

Costa: Never found a remarkable one yet. Sorry. They're all friendly, competent and pleasant, but never distinguished.

Crussh: Surprise your friends by leading them into 4 Millbank (SW1P 3JA), a posh-looking office complex used for political television broadcasts. To the left of the lobby is a largely hidden branch of this juice and salad bar, devoid of tourists and with free Wi-Fi and laptop charge points.

Pret: The omnipresent sandwich shop does pretty decent coffee for a chain, but tends to be the most uniform across its branches. All exposed brick and wooden surfaces – at least they've stopped playing that infernal light jazz that was once a limiting factor on one's tolerance. What Pret lacks in character, it makes up for in space. The main Victoria branch, for example, has a huge upstairs seating area that is a champion spot for freelancers to linger with their laptops.

An increasing number of smaller chains are muscling in on the market, but I'd better stop there before I'm lynched for supporting evil corporates.

5 pm

A BRIDGE INTO EVENING

The fifth hour of the afternoon is a funny time: a transition time. The city is yet to hit full rush hour, but everyone is thinking about it. These 60 minutes connect the lazy afternoon to the frenetic pace of early evening. A bridging time. And a good time to punningly consider the city's bridges.

For most of London's history, there were only three ways to cross the Thames: by boat, by swimming (not advised) or by the hideously log-jammed London Bridge. A crossing has existed at the site of London Bridge, on and off, since Roman times. It was only in the 18th century that other crossings in central London joined it, beginning with Westminster Bridge in 1750. Between Vauxhall and Tower Bridges there are now ten ways to get across on foot. And I'm going to tell you something you probably don't know about all of them.

VAUXHALL BRIDGE

Look over the side of this bridge and you might just see a miniature St Paul's. One of the female sculptures adorning the sides clutches a replica of the cathedral.

Bonus fact: In the Bond film *Skyfall* (2012), M is driving across the bridge when she witnesses an explosion at her MI6 office, on the south side of the bridge.

LAMBETH BRIDGE

Note the colour of this span. The red hue is intended to match the colour scheme of the House of Lords, at the nearest end of the Houses of Parliament. If you now look up stream to the paint job on Westminster Bridge, and then visualise the House of Commons, you'll note a similar correspondence.

Bonus fact: Lambeth is a medieval name, meaning 'landing place [on the river] for lambs'.

WESTMINSTER BRIDGE

The first bridge to be built in the capital since the medieval London Bridge, the original Westminster Bridge opened in 1750. It might have gone up 100 years earlier, had it not been stymied by angry boatmen, who feared they could lose their trade as a result.

Bonus fact: Cross the bridge around noon on the southern pathway. On a sunny day, the trefoil patterning on the balustrades casts rather lewd-shaped shadows onto the pavement.

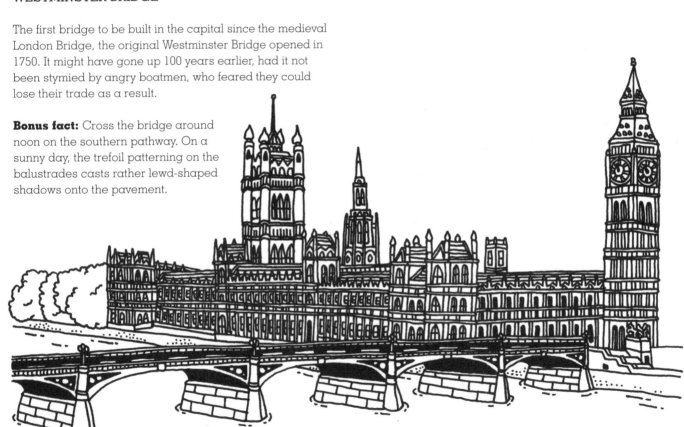

GOLDEN JUBILEE FOOTBRIDGES

The original suspension bridge here was designed by Isambard Kingdom Brunel. The sturdy piers and lower brickwork are all that remains of his bridge, though the cabling was reused on the Clifton Suspension Bridge.

Bonus fact: Look over the pier on the eastern side of the bridge to see a skateboard graveyard. Skaters who wreck their decks at the nearby Southbank Skatepark use this pier as a final resting place for their boards.

WATERLOO BRIDGE

This used to be known as the Ladies' Bridge, on account of the often-asserted notion that it was built by a female workforce during the Second World War. Few realise it, but the architect is none other than Giles Gilbert Scott, who also gave us Tate Modern, Battersea Power Station and the red phone box.

Bonus fact: The bridge was the scene of one of London's oddest murders. In 1978, Bulgarian dissident Georgi Markov was shot with a ricin-filled pellet, fired from a gun disguised as an umbrella.

BLACKFRIARS BRIDGE

This rubicund crossing was opened by Queen Victoria on the very same morning as nearby Holborn Viaduct. Take a look – they have similar stylings. The oddity here though is the decoration: you'll find bird sculptures lurking in the capitals along each side. Those facing downriver, towards the estuary, are seabirds. Those facing upriver, towards the source of the Thames, are freshwater birds. The arrangement is said to represent the point along the river where the waters have a saline content halfway between pure river and sea. I've never been able to get anyone in authority to confirm this, however, so take it with a pinch of, ahem, salt.

Bonus fact: The northern part of the structure contains a rifle range.

MILLENNIUM BRIDGE

The pedestrian-only span linking St Paul's and Tate Modern is affectionately referred to as the 'wobbly bridge'. When it first opened in 1999, the rhythm of the footfall set up oscillations in the structure, causing it to sway disconcertingly. The fault was soon fixed.

Bonus fact: The futuristic curves of the bridge were put to unlikely use in the film *Guardians of the Galaxy* (2014), where it doubles as a bridge on the planet Xander.

SOUTHWARK BRIDGE

Perhaps the only bridge on the Thames to have blown up. Sort of. In February 1895, a 1.5m (5ft) section of the span exploded, injuring four people. The accident was caused by faulty wiring for street lighting.

Bonus fact: This is the only central London bridge to contain all the vowels.

LONDON BRIDGE

The modern, unmemorable bridge was built in the 1960s to replace an 1830s structure (now in America), which itself replaced the famous medieval bridge. London Bridge was the site of the worst tragedy in London's history, which hardly anybody today has heard about. In 1212, Londoners flocked onto the bridge to watch the progress of a fire in Southwark. A change in the wind blew embers across the river, starting a fire at the northern end of the bridge. Hundreds of people became trapped on the span. We will never know how many people lost their lives to flame, smoke, crush or drowning, but some sources estimate it was as many as 3,000.

Bonus fact: The modern bridge is, in fact, hollow. It's possible to walk across through the chambers beneath the roadway.

TOWER BRIDGE

London's most famous bridge, though often confused with London Bridge. Its history is well documented, including the incident in 1952, when bus driver Albert Gunter jumped his double decker bus over the gap, as the bascules of the bridge opened. Less well known are the daredevils who piloted planes beneath the bridge. The first was in 1912, when Frank McClean flew a seaplane beneath this and many other Thames bridges just nine years after the Wright Brothers' pioneering flight. The last to do so was a jet fighter in 1968. The pilot had no permission and was protesting his dissatisfaction at the RAF.

Bonus fact: Each of the lifting bascules weighs around 1,000 tons.

6 pm
PUBS

When we think of London culture, it is perhaps the theatres, museums, galleries or historic buildings that dominate the mental tableau. Yet the London pub deserves pre-eminence in the cultural constellation. Not only do pubs provide top-notch food and drink, but many double up as theatres, museums, galleries and historic buildings in their own right. A mid-afternoon tipple is best if you simply want to enjoy your surroundings, but 6pm is when the pub comes to life.

TYPES OF PUB

London is particularly rich in pubs we might describe as '**Ye Olde**'. These are establishments that have history, or like to think that they do. Such places typically contain a warren of rooms or partitioned areas, making each visit a different experience. Unsurprisingly, these pubs tend to cluster in the older parts of town, especially Holborn and the City.

A Locals pub might ultimately be defined as a pub with lots of local people in it, rather than one with a transient passing trade. The term implies so much more, though. A dubious smelling carpet, a rarely troubled dartboard with faded chalk scoring, an easy conversation with a stranger, a dearth of ales in favour of mega-brewery lagers: all are hallmarks of a stereotypical 'Locals' pub. You'll find them in Zones 2 outwards, with the occasional interloper in Zone 1.

The Gastropub is any pub that serves food as a main attraction – in some cases, *the* main attraction. It is perfectly reasonable to content yourself with nothing more than a drink – preferably wine – but you might feel a little awkward about it. Sometimes you get table service, sometimes you must venture to the bar, and always you will assume wrongly and make a fist of ordering.

The Bar-pub styles itself like a pub, often with a good old authentic name like 'The Holborn Whippet' or 'Mother Kelly's'. Yet inside, the walls are stark, the bar area minimalist. This 'We're a pub but we don't look like a pub' idea is on the rise, especially at venues that specialise in craft ales. It's not uncommon for the taps or pumps to lack any branding, and the nonplussed drinker must consult a menu board to choose their tipple.

The Events pub London's pubs have never been solely about drinking. They've long served as places for impromptu business meetings, political gatherings and musical entertainment. In Georgian times, the local pub was often used for coroner's enquiries or even criminal trials. The tradition carries on today with many drinking dens staging live music, variety evenings or intellectual discussions. There's also a thriving community of meet-up groups, who gather in pubs to discuss everything from French literature to life on other planets. All classes of pub dabble in this area, but some make a speciality of hiring out function rooms to bring like-minded people, often strangers, together.

Makeover pubs are another growing phenomenon. Here, some grand but defunct building is recalled to life as a place to enjoy a drink. Former theatres, banking halls, working men's clubs, department stores, even a tram shed, are stripped, refitted and opened to drinkers. The Wetherspoon chain was a pioneer of this type, with dozens of examples across London. More recently, the Antic group has persuaded us that, yes, we really do want to drink in an old department store named after a local brothel keeper. Mismatched furniture is a must, for some reason.

The Also-rans are the perfectly decent boozers that do everything well but nothing exceptionally well. Such pubs are legion and represent the typical London boozer. Anywhere with brass fittings, plastic menu cards, and those tedious white salt-shakers on every table will probably fit this category. These are the haunts of old-guard brewers like Fullers, Youngs and Greene King (though all have some excellent venues in other categories). Again, you'll probably have a great time in these places, but the word 'bedazzled' will not suggest itself.

LONDON'S BEST PUBS

Estimates vary depending on definitions, but it seems there are around 7,000 pubs in London. I reckon I've visited around 1,000, and could fill a book as long as this one with recommendations. What follows, though, is a distillation of absolute, must-visit pubs. I've started with some well-known central venues, for majority convenience, but I've also included a fair few commendable places a little further out.

CENTRAL

The Blackfriar
174 Queen Victoria Street, EC4V 4EG (Blackfriars)

Have you ever seen anything like it? A wedge of a pub decorated with grinning monks and Art Nouveau flourishes. Head inside and the gaudy decorations are marinaded into the walls, a friar tucked into every corner. The vaulted dining area is the most overblown refectory this side of the V&A. Still, it's impossible not to love The Blackfriar, especially when you discover the adventurous ale selection. This is the unofficial waiting room for Blackfriars train station, and you'll often overhear punters decrying the 'Bloody Thameslink'.

Cittie of Yorke
22 High Holborn, WC1V 6BN (Blackfriars)

I have to declare a bias. As an alumnus of York I naturally gravitated to this pub, despite its inept spelling, on my first arrival. I've never had a bad night here, though. The main bar is unique – a long, tall hall with huge vats pendant from the walls. It all looks like a ship's engine room, complete with snugs that resemble mariners' bunks, to one side. A secondary room is kitted out like a Georgian drawing room, while the ancient stone basement is quite a find. I swear there's a hidden beer garden here too, but it never seems to be open, and no one believes me.

Princess Louise
208 High Holborn, WC1V 7EP (Holborn)

This is the picture-book example of a Victorian gin palace. You'll adore the partitioned drinking spaces, the intricately etched glass and mirrored bar area, even if much of it is modern retro-artifice. The Princess's charms can be her undoing, at least for those seeking a quiet drink. The handsome ground-floor bar is perpetually thronged, even mid-afternoon. Head upstairs for a lesser but quieter space. Head downstairs for some Grade II listed urinals – worth a sneak peek even if you have no business being in the gents'

toilet. If you're prepared to venture further, Maida Vale's **Prince Alfred** (5a Formosa Street, W9 1EE) offers something very similar and perhaps even more opulent.

Ye Olde Cheshire Cheese
145 Fleet Street, EC4A 2BU (Chancery Lane)

The *sine qua non* of any historic pub tour, the Cheese somehow gets to be both a tourist bar AND an essential experience for proper Londoners. I've visited some three dozen times over the years, and I swear I'll find a new room every time. If Harry Potter ever grew out of that wretched butterbeer and craved an enchanted boozer in which to get lashed, he would choose this place. The Sam Smith's beer is not to everyone's taste, but it's cheap and its really the atmosphere you're here for.

EAST

The Well and Bucket
143 Bethnal Green Road, E2 7DG (Shoreditch High Street)

A Victorian original, which hung up its tankards a few decades ago to become a clothing outlet, the Well and Bucket recently came out of retirement and is serving ales again. And how. The busy bar dispenses all manner of lesser-spotted brews, be it draught, keg or bottle. The food, too, is superb, but never muscles out the drinking ethos of the place. A scrappy little beer garden, some truly memorable artwork and a cosy basement cocktail bar suggest a confused establishment, but its one you can easily fall for. The small Barworks chain runs other pubs on the City fringes, such as the recenty opended **Singer Tavern** (1 City Road, EC2A 1AN) and the **Electricity Showrooms** (39a Hoxton Square, N1 6NN). All are worth seeking out.

The Blind Beggar
337 Whitechapel Road, E1 1BU (Whitechapel)

Yeah, it's the place where one of the Krays murdered a rival. That's all very impressive/depressing, but also very well known. Less well known is that the Beggar is a surprisingly characterful pub with a real mix of locals, morbid tourists and sports fans. Gangland lore aside, this place gets a thumbs up for (a) having an excellent pool table, and (b) the pool of another kind in the beer garden, which supports a school of chunky koi carp. Order a plate of fish and chips, observe the koi, and contemplate your mortality in this pub of death. Oh, and the almost neighbouring White Hart is also worth a look.

SOUTH

The George Inn
75–77 Borough High Street, SE1 1NH (London Bridge)

This is another very well known pub, but one impossible to leave out of a listing such as this. The George revels in its status as 'London's only remaining coaching inn'; that is, a place where stagecoaches would rest overnight before the final squeeze across the medieval London Bridge. So historic is this place that it has its own biography (a witty book called *Shakespeare's Local* by Pete Brown), and the landlord is the National Trust. Don't expect good phone reception: the pub is supposedly haunted by the landlady who presided over The George at the time when the railways arrived, taking all her coaching custom. Her spectre hates any new technology, and regularly screws over anything that looks like progress.

Catford Constitutional Club
Catford Broadway, SE6 4SP (Catford Bridge)

Not so much 'This shouldn't work, but it does' as 'This shouldn't work, but it damn well makes me want to get down on my knees and whoop with delight'. The triple-C is bloody scary from the outside: a tumbledown building in an unfashionable area that looks like the sort of place in which the music will cut out the second you walk through the door – assuming the electricity's actually working and the door isn't barred. But once inside, it's a superb example of the Antic chain's ability to take an old building and renew it with wonder. Interesting beers, questionable non-decor and a damn fine kitchen all make this so much more memorable (in a good way) than the typical pub. There are many similar examples from this chain across town that I might equally have listed (**Balham Bowls Club**, 7–9 Ramsden Road, SW12 8QX and **The Tooting Tram and Social**, 46–48 Mitcham Road, SW17 9NA, for example, self-explain their origins). Make a list and go tick them all off.

The Ship
41 Jews Row, SW18 1TB (Wandsworth Town)

Talk about an odd location. The Ship nestles on the semi-industrial edge of Wandsworth, directly above a sewage outfall pipe. That this was voted one of the best gastropubs in the country is therefore especially wonderful. And yet the pub has the good grace to wear its culinary achievements with little ostentation. The main dining area is hidden well away from the various spaces where drinkers can get on with the more important business of sipping beer. There's a definite maritime flavour about the older, original bar, recapitulated in the beer

garden where you'll find life buoys, ships' wheels and other macronauticalia.

WEST

The Dove
19 Upper Mall, W6 9TA (Hammersmith)

A pleasant, peaceful retreat in the riverine reaches of Hammersmith. The Dove reckons to have one of the smallest bars in the Kingdom, which I would dispute if only I could get in. There are larger rooms to the back, though, and a particularly fine riverside terrace arranged on two layers. Cosy in the winter, attractive in the summer, this is one of London's finest all-rounders.

Dragonfly Brewery
183 High Street, W3 9DJ (Acton Town)

Acton finally becomes a destination with this superb pub of two halves. In the front, you get the dark wood atmosphere of the ancient George and Dragon pub. Round the back, you'll find the towering copper fermenters of the new brewery. They brew some mighty good stuff, and there are few finer interiors in which to enjoy a smart swig.

NORTH

The Holly Bush
22 Holly Mount, NW3 6SG (Hampstead)

Any guide that covers Hampstead will tell you to go to the **Spaniard's Inn** for a drink. Well, it's certainly a gem, but so far from any tube station. Plus, I have it on good authority that the Spaniard's numerous ghost stories were entirely made up in the 1980s by a previous landlord. So, instead, head to Holly Mount, where this attractive hilltop pub will charm your socks off (if the serious gradients don't wear them out first). I once spied Noel Gallagher in here, which might be a ringing endorsement or a clinching off-putter, depending on your proclivities.

The Pineapple
51 Leverton Street, NW5 2NX (Kentish Town)

Kentish Town has an embarrassment of riches when it comes to good pubs. Craft-aleheads will already know the

Southampton Arms (139 Highgate Road, NW5 1LE). Gastro-seekers can admire the **Bull & Last** (168 Highgate Road, NW5 1QS). There are at least six other nearby boozers that I'd say are worth an hour of anyone's time. The Pineapple, though, is the best all-rounder. The backstreet boozer has a strong local following, favouring a younger crowd but welcoming to all. Its beer range, while not quite as staggering as the Southampton, is still superb and regularly supplemented by mini-festivals in the small back garden. If only I lived nearby, 80 per cent of this book would have been written in The Pineapple. It's that good.

AT THIS HOUR:

Gresham College is one of the oldest educational institutions in London, dating back to Tudor times. It puts on free public lectures two or three times a week on every subject from stellar astronomy to political reform to peculiar mathematics. The talks take place either at lunchtime or 6pm, often at the college's historic Barnard's Inn Hall in Holborn (EC1N 2HH).

7 pm

EVENING ENTERTAINMENT

Having lubricated your system with a refreshing beverage, it's time to seek out some evening entertainment.

THE WEST END

It hardly needs to be said that London's West End is one of the world's most famous districts for theatre and live performance. Indeed, the area is so well established, and so well publicised that it really needs no further introduction here, other than a few tips from me.

Big West End shows are among the most in-demand experiences one can have in London. Tickets are booked up early, and often command a high fee. It's worth looking out for deals if you're not restricted to a particular date or time. Every year, for example, the Society of London Theatre puts on its Get Into London Theatre promotion, which offers discounted tickets for shows in the relatively quiet season of January and February. Savings range from 20–60 per cent, with some seats available for as little as £10. The deals cover just about every West End show, from small short-run plays to blockbusters like *The Lion King*. Various websites also offer deals, although they are usually aimed at out-of-towners.

Opera can be even pricier than the conventional stage, with some tickets racking up at £200. If you book early, and are prepared to stand or suffer a restricted view, however, you can get into a Royal Opera House production for a tenner. Both that house, and the English National Opera on St

Martin's Lane offer same-day tickets at much discounted prices, but these are rapidly snapped up.

FRINGE THEATRE

For the best of London theatre, look beyond the big shows. Fringe theatre can, of course, be highly variable in quality. But choose wisely and you'll hit the jackpot. The small stage can be found in many quarters of town. Some of the best lurk above or behind pubs. Try, for example, **The Gatehouse** in Highgate (Highgate Village, N6 4BD). This theatre has the unique attribute of sitting on the border of three London boroughs. More centrally, the **Old Red Lion** on St John Street (418 St John Street, EC1V 4NJ), the **Hen and Chickens** at Highbury Circus (109 St Paul's Road, N1 2NA), and the **Lion & Unicorn** in Kentish Town (42–44 Gaisford Street, NW5 2ED) are all good examples. Head out west, meanwhile, for **The Orange Tree** in Richmond (45 Kew Road, TW9 2NQ), which has London's only permanent 'in-the-round' stage.

In the summer time, **The Scoop** performance space outside City Hall (The Queen's Walk, SE1 2AA) puts on free theatrical productions, from Shakespeare to contemporary plays. You'll also find cinema screenings here.

One of London's most beautiful theatres is hidden away in Shadwell, well off the tourist track. **Wilton's Music Hall** (1 Graces Alley, E1 8JB) is exceptionally atmospheric, a stalwart survivor from the age of Marie Lloyd. With walls that look like they haven't seen a lick of paint since one of the Edwards sat on the throne, and barley-twist columns that appear too fragile to hold up the mezzanine, this is a unique place indeed. Book tickets for a show, or simply pop in to sample the candle-lit bar. The only other place remotely like Wilton's is **Hoxton Hall**, a mile or two away (130 Hoxton Street, N1 6SH). This, too, is an old music hall with bags of character, with regular fringe theatre shows.

IMMERSIVE ENTERTAINMENT

Punchdrunk
Various locations.

One of the great theatrical revolutions of the past half-decade is for 'immersive theatre', or 'promenade theatre'. Here, the audience are not passive spectators watching a stage, but active participants of the show. The genre is epitomised by the Punchdrunk company, who put on utterly spellbinding performances that see you clambering through secret passages, joining hands with strangers, and perhaps even being pulled into a side room for an argument, or a snog. It can be terrifying, exhilarating and liberating, but never boring. I have a friend who went to one show over 30 times: nobody ever says that about *The Mousetrap*. Part of the charm of such ventures is that the location is 'site-specific' – perhaps a warehouse or an old industrial building – so there's no particular venue to recommend. Other companies are now rapidly catching up with Punchdrunk, so check listings sites for regular tip-offs.

The Vaults
Leake Street, SE1 7NN (Waterloo)

The Vaults, beneath Waterloo station, is one of the few locations that regularly puts on something of this ilk. The warren of old railway arches and tunnels is ideal for anything a little macabre or gothic, and it pays to keep an eye on their programme. At the time of writing, upcoming events include a *Zombie Blitz* and *Alice's Adventures Underground*.

Secret Cinema
Various locations.

Other genres, too, have taken this site-specific approach. Secret Cinema, founded in 2007, screens big movies in unusual, often appropriate locations. *One Flew Over The*

Cuckoo's Nest, for example, was screened in a derelict hospital, while *The Grand Budapest Hotel* took over a suitably grand warehouse building in Clerkenwell. Attendees often don't know what the film is until they get there – hence 'secret'.

COMEDY

London remains the world centre of cutting-edge comedy, with dozens of venues putting on nightly shows. **The Comedy Store** (1a Oxenden Street, SW1Y 4EE) remains the city's biggest temple to the chuckling arts. It offers at least one show every day, using the traditional format of multiple short performances. The nearby **Soho Theatre** (21 Dean Street, W1D 3NE) specialises in one-act shows, giving comedians time and space to deliver longer sets.

Not all the best comedy is hogged by the centre of town, however. **The Angel Comedy Club** above the Camden Head pub (2 Camden Passage, N1 8DY) fills up every night for a free show. The venue should not be confused with **The Camden Head** (100 Camden High Street, NW1 0LU), whose tiny upstairs room has played host to such luminaries as Stewart Lee, Alan Carr, Russell Howard and… me (ludicrously wrapped in tin foil for a space-themed gig). The whole area goes stand-up mad each August, as the Camden Fringe gives comedians a chance to try out material for Edinburgh.

London's oldest-running comedy club is south of the river in Greenwich. **Up The Creek** (302 Creek Road, SE10 9SW) was founded in 1991 by Malcolm Hardee, the man credited with inventing the phrase 'alternative comedy'. It still puts on top shows every weekend, followed by a disco.

GO TO A TALK

To some, the idea of going to a lecture might seem dry, worthy and the very last thing one might expect to find in a guidebook section called 'Evening Entertainment'. That would be a shame. London is a world leader in this respect with dozens of venues offering free or cheap access to some of the world's most erudite minds. I could fill a book on such places, but here's a selection that spans some of the great variety in formats. Note that times may vary, but 7pm is typical of most.

The Lost Lectures
Various mystery locations

The site-specific lead pioneered by the likes of Punchdrunk and Secret Cinema is increasingly spilling over into other

AT THIS HOUR:

Royal Observatory, Greenwich, has an impressive nocturnal trick. Every night, from 4pm until midnight, it fires a laser beam northwards along the Meridian Line. To see it, you need to be somewhere along that line, or within a few hundred feet either side: Greenwich riverfront, or the area around the O2 arena are also good options.

forms of entertainment. The Lost Lectures uses a mystery venue to put on short, punchy talks by unusual characters, lubricated by quirky musical acts and a general party vibe. The sessions take place every few months – one previous show made use of a forgotten ballroom in Alexandra Palace – with previous speakers including Carol Ann Duffy, Ruby Wax and Simon Singh.

The Royal Institution
21 Albemarle Street, W1S 4BS (Green Park)

With its stuccoed Corinthian facade and unhelpfully ambiguous name, the RI can seem a little off-putting if you've never stepped inside before. It is, however, an unquenchable source of discovery and curiosity. Famously, ten chemical elements were discovered in this building, and 14 Nobel Prizes have been awarded to its scientists. These and other stories are told in its small basement museum, but this is first and foremost an arena for public talks from top scientists. You might recognise the plush auditorium from the RI's televised Christmas Lectures, the selfsame stage upon which Michael Faraday wowed Victorian audiences. Today, you can expect the likes of Brian Cox, Alice Roberts and Steven Pinker to fill that space. Literally marvellous.

London School of Economics
Houghton Street, WC2A 2AE (Temple or Holborn)

You can practically get a free education in the social sciences from LSE, such is the calibre and frequency of its free public lectures. The university attracts speakers from all over the globe, including world leaders and well-known politicians, to its stage. This is an immense public service that doesn't get the wide recognition it deserves. What's more, the organisers are on the ball when it comes to dissemination. Nearly all events are filmed and put on to YouTube, with a suggested hashtag to get conversation going on Twitter.

Thinking Bob
Various locations (https://www.thinkingbob.co.uk)

Thinking Bob is representative of a growing trend for meetup groups that attract like-minded individuals to the same place for a drink, natter and usually a talk or quiz. There are many examples to be found on sites like meetup.com, but this group seems to be growing faster than most. Events include a debate about whether debate is dead, a walking talk/tour/sampler around Borough Market and a popular night where you do the talking, on random themes... to strangers.

8 pm

DINNER OUT

London is now seen as one of the world's great culinary cities, thanks to its thriving restaurant scene. It would take a book several times the girth of this one even to approach a comprehensive list. I offer instead my own selection of the more inventive, impressive or characterful places to eat out of an evening.

CENTRAL

Inamo
134–136 Wardour Street, W1F 8ZP (Tottenham Court Road)

Inamo in Soho has one unique selling point that sets it apart from the now-uncountable number of Japanese restaurants in central London. Your menu is projected on to the table in front of you. Clever sensors track your hand movements, allowing you to order food and drinks, attract the waiting staff, pay your bill, or even play arcade games with the person sat opposite. One can image a future historian, living in an age when holograms are everywhere, pointing back to places like this, and saying how far-sighted they were.

Dans le Noir?
30–31 Clerkenwell Green, EC1R 0DU (Farringdon)

Dans le Noir? is for anyone who rails against pretentious presentation. As anyone with even the most basic level of French can intuit from the restaurant's name, you won't see your food at all. The dining room is kept in darkness while blind or partially sighted waiting staff fulfil your order. Here, too, you're kept in the dark. You select a type of food and alert staff to your dietary needs, but you have no idea exactly what they'll serve you. Yes, it's gimmicky, but it's thought-provoking.

NORTH

Poppies Fish and Chips
30 Hawley Crescent, NW1 8NP (Camden Town)

Despite a preponderance of international cuisine, there's no denying the continued popularity of the humble chippy. Perhaps the most famous, and deservedly so, is Poppies, a traditional fish and chip shop with Spitalfields origins, but now trading from a second branch in Camden Town. I once began a bizarre project to weigh the haddock and chips from multiple vendors and divide by cost to find the best-value-for-money grub in town. Poppies won by some margin, and also came up trumps on taste. The Camden branch brings more glam to this already winning formula with a 40s jukebox and free live music on Friday and Saturday nights.

Dishoom
5 Stable Street, N1C 4AB (King's Cross St Pancras)

Unlike many of the restaurants in this list, Dishoom has no particular gimmick or unusual venue. It doesn't need one. The enormous dining room and bar can seat hundreds (and there's more in the basement), but the former warehouse space still feels cosy and intimate. The food – a modern take on Indian classics – will appeal to both vegetarians and meat eaters. While you're in the area, the neighbouring **Grain Store** (1–3 Stable Street N1C 4AB) and **Caravan** (1 Granary Building, Granary Square N1C 4AA) are also highly recommended. What a change this former railway land has seen in the past three years.

SOUTH

Skylon
Royal Festival Hall, Belvedere Road, SE1 8XX (Waterloo)

The book you're reading was inspired by a 1951 guide to London, coinciding with the Festival of Britain. It would be remiss, therefore, to exclude Skylon – a restaurant named after that festival's most famous landmark. It is situated inside the only surviving building from the post-war extravaganza. As such, it offers pleasant views of the Thames and Waterloo Bridge. The menu is pleasingly simple, with main courses named simply 'beef' or 'cheese' or 'halibut', but the quality of cheffing is exceptional. Skylon is a true destination restaurant rather than the half-hearted tourist trap that could so easily have been yawned into existence in this spot.

Dosa n Chutny
68 Tooting High Street, SW17 0RN (Tooting Broadway)

I was first led here following a rather indulgent tour of a local brewery. On first spying the unassuming restaurant, I assumed we were just choosing any old food outlet to soak up the booze. How wrong I was. Dosa n Chutny specialises in south Indian food, particularly from the Chennai region. The menu is of epic length and unimpeachable quality. Most head straight for the titular dosas, which come in 20 different varieties, but I'm a sucker for paneer curry, which again can be ordered in multiple styles. If you're not drinking, you can easily enjoy a two-course meal for less than a tenner.

EAST

La Chapelle
3 Spital Square, E1 6DY (Liverpool Street)

You can scarcely imagine the splendours inside this eastern outpost of the Galvin empire. From the outside, the Grade II-listed hall is almost invisible, skulking behind the company's more modern bistro building. Within, you're dining in what used to be a church hall and school building. Elegantly set tables nestle beneath a wood-beamed pitched roof, while a modern glass mezzanine somehow complements the Victorian splendour. This is top French cuisine, with a vast wine list and sommelier service. Despite the Gallic reputation for carnivorous dining, La Chapelle has an excellent respect for vegetarians, including a seven-course Menu Gourmand.

Hill & Szrok
60 Broadway Market, E8 4QJ (London Fields)

The best restaurants always source their meat from a quality local butcher. With Hill & Szrok, the supply chain is a matter of inches. By day, Mr Hill runs the building as a master butcher's. In the evening, the meats are moved to chef Szrok's kitchen and the setting transmogrifies into a small restaurant. The venue remains trendy, and takes no bookings, so be prepared to queue for some of the best meat you'll find anywhere.

WEST

Harwood Arms
Walham Grove, SW6 1QP (Fulham Broadway)

I'd like to introduce something called Brown's Gastroscale, which places pubs on a linear gradation from 1 (no food served, not even crisps and nuts) to 10 (consummate gastropub). The Harwood would adhere limpet-like to the right-hand edge of that scale. It is, quite simply, king of the gastropubs, and even boasts a Michelin star. It looks like a pub, but what boozer serves 'Rolled rabbit terrine with prunes cooked in Earl Grey, turnip and almonds'? A craft ale or two is available on draught, but the wine list reads like a viticultural novella with over 200 options. It's pricey – three courses cost around £40 – but sets a standard for pub dining unmatched elsewhere in the capital.

Daquise
20 Thurloe Street, SW7 2LT (South Kensington)

This timeless Polish restaurant has been in business since the 1940s, selling classic East European cuisine to the grateful masses. It has some history, supposedly serving as a favoured meet-up spot for Cold War spies, and also keeping Roman Polanski topped up with goulash. It's spartan but welcoming and, with a basement overspill, much bigger than it appears. I've chosen it for sentimental reasons, however. This was the first London restaurant I ever visited as an adult, and the stodgy cabbage, beef and dumpling concoctions were reminiscent of the stews I'd left behind in Yorkshire.

9 pm

A COCKTAIL OR TWO

It's official: London is the best place to drink on the planet. Every year the World's 50 Best Bars Awards ranks the globe's cocktail elite. Every year, London comes up trumps. In 2014, our city claimed eight spots in that top 50, more than any other location. Three were in the top ten.

CENTRAL

The Artesian
The Langham, Portland Place, W1B 1JA (Oxford Circus)

And the winner of best bar in 2014 was the Artesian, which had also triumphed in 2013 and 2012. This is the venue favoured by Lady Gaga whenever she's in town. It is the very room in which the second Sherlock Holmes story *The Sign of Four* and Oscar Wilde's *Picture of Dorian Grey* were commissioned, at what must have been the most important editorial meeting of all time. It also holds a no-reservations policy, so you simply turn up and drink. Expect to pay £15–£20 for a cocktail but, trust me, it'll be an experience you'll remember. Captured clouds, obfuscating mirrors and the smell of opium all featured on my last visit.

Bassoon Bar
Corinthia Hotel, 10 Whitehall Place, SW1A 2BD (Embankment)

Another classy (though expensive) option can be found in the Corinthia Hotel in Westminster. Any of its bars can be recommended, but the Bassoon Bar is the most relaxing and sophisticated. Its cocktails average around £16, but for that you get to enjoy the suave Art Deco interiors, the promise of live music (from Tuesday and Saturday) and the charms of an historic building that was a hub of overseas espionage during the Second World War.

The Cocktail Trading Co.
22 Great Marlborough Street, W1F 7HU (Oxford Circus)

One of the hottest new openings in London, and already winner of some fine trophies, is The Cocktail Trading Co. near Carnaby Street, which is making waves with customers and within the industry, where it doubles as a training academy for would-be drink makers. Three award-winning bartenders mix up playful, experimental drinks. Expect your cocktail to arrive in a noodle box, or a ceramic wellington boot, or anything at all, really. Superb bellinis, too.

The Bar
Courthouse Hotel, 19–21 Great Marlborough Street, W1F 7HL (Oxford Circus)

Right next to The Cocktail Trading Co. is a very different proposition. I include The Bar at the Courthouse not because it does the best cocktails, but for the unique decor. The hotel bar contains three prison cells, complete with toilets and beds, from the days when this was indeed a courthouse. You can sit in the cells, sipping an espresso martini, imagining that you're Mick Jagger, Johnny Rotten, or any of the other rock stars that passed through the courts back in the day. Stick your head into the restaurant, too, for more judicial throwbacks.

Donovan Bar
Brown's Hotel, 30-34 Albemarle Street, W1S 4BP (Green Park)

I must surely recommend Brown's Hotel in Mayfair, not only because it shares my surname, but also for its history. From this building, the first telephone call in Britain was made by Alexander Graham Bell in 1876. His apparatus is still there, and can usually be viewed if you ask the concierge nicely. Otherwise, head to the hotel's Donovan Bar, a homage to 1960s London and photographer Terence Donovan. If you're in luck, they'll seat you in the 'naughty corner', which is decorated with some of Donovan's more candid shots (to be honest, they're not all that risque).

The Fumoir
Claridge's, 49 Brook Street, W1K 4HR (Bond Street)

The final word in high-end sophistication, with its rich leather and velvet furnishings and muted Art Deco flourishes. The bar is tiny and operates a no-reservations policy, so you have to time your visit carefully. This all means that, if you can get in, you're likely to be sharing the intimate space with the rich, the glamorous and the famous.

The London Gin Club
The Star at Night, 22 Great Chapel Street, W1F 8FR (Tottenham Court Road)

Fans of a good G&T need look no further than the laid-back London Gin Club. Things looked bleak for the former Star at Night pub when a huge Crossrail dig cut off most of the passing trade. Julia, the owner, hit upon the wheeze of turning the place into a gin palace, and she hasn't looked back since. You probably never realised there were so many types of gin – or tonic – but the friendly staff will readily help you navigate. Julia's also something of an aficionado for the history of London, so be sure to have a natter.

A CHARLOTTE STREET QUARTET

Bourne & Hollingsworth
28 Rathbone Place, W1T 1JF (Goodge Street)
The Reverend JW Simpson
32 Goodge Street, W1T 2QJ (Goodge Street)
Shochu Lounge
Roka, 37 Charlotte Street, W1T 1RR (Goodge Street)
The Red Bar
Bam-Bou, 1 Percy Street, W1T 1DB (Goodge Street)

Across the great divide of Oxford Street and into Fitzrovia, you'll find most of the best bars grouped around Charlotte Street. Bourne & Hollingsworth, named after a long-defunct department store, was one of the original speakeasy-style basement bars to spark this now crowded scene. Their tiny bar is decked out like your great aunt's sitting room, with floral wallpaper and lampshades a-go-go, which makes for an oddly enjoyable vibe. The same company also runs trendy dive bar The Reverend JW Simpson on nearby Goodge Street, accessed via an anonymous black door. For a taste of the east, Shochu Lounge offers a lot more space than your typical basement bar, and is one of the best places in London to try shochu, a Japanese spirit distilled from barley. Finally, in this most intense of cocktail quarters, try The Red Bar at Bam-Bou. This place turns the basement bar idea on its head by instead running from the top floor. The drinks menu is extensive and full of exotic names, including what's thought to be the best range of Japanese whisky in the UK.

Bar Polski
11 Little Turnstile, WC1V 7DX (Holborn)

After all this sophistication, the wonderful Bar Polski is refreshingly down to earth. As you might guess, its speciality is vodka, proffered in a bewildering number of flavours for about £3 a shot. The place always feels a little chaotic, but

the friendly bar staff – who've been here since forever – are supremely efficient. Order a tray of three random shots, wish your friends 'na zdowie' (which, if memory serves, was the former name of this bar), and make jokes about the massive cock on the wall.

EAST

A SHOREDITCH TRIO

Nightjar
129 City Road, EC1V 1JB (Old Street)
Happiness Forgets
Basement, 8-9 Hoxton Square, N1 6NU (Old Street)
Callooh Callay
65 Rivington Street, EC2A 3AY (Shoreditch High Street)

Shoreditch, with the neighbouring areas of Hoxton and Spitalfields, remains the undisputed kingdom of the cocktail. Here you'll find this established and still deservedly popular trio – all of which gained top 20 places at the most recent World's Best Bars awards, along with relative newcomer **White Lyan** (153–155 Hoxton Street, N1 6PJ). All have regularly changing cocktail menus, largely crafted in-house by ingenious mixologists. It's the little touches that stick in

the memory, though: the menu in an Oyster Card holder at Callooh Callay, for example. **Nightjar** has now reached a level of popularity where you must book several days in advance to gain entry through its anonymous City Road door. This is the archetypal basement bar, with cosy leather banquettes, dim lighting and creative cocktails that might arrive in Toby jugs or kettles. Round the corner, **Happiness Forgets** offers a similar subterranean experience, laced with a more traditional Shoreditch vibe of exposed brickwork and bar stools. **Callooh Callay** is the biggest of the three, and not confined to a basement. The trick is to get an invitation through the wardrobe, and emerge Narnia-like into the back bar.

The Mayor of Scaredy Cat Town
Breakfast Club, 12–16 Artillery Lane, E1 7LS (Liverpool Street)

The strangest gimmick of all (not to mention the name) can surely be found at The Mayor of Scaredy Cat Town, a 'secret' bar in the basement of the Spitalfields Breakfast Club. To gain entry, you must enquire if the Mayor is at home. You are then ushered *through a Smeg fridge* to a hidden staircase, which leads down to a small basement bar. A good one to show out-of-town friends just how crazy London can be.

AND THE REST...

The Worship Street Whistling Shop
63 Worship Street, EC2A 2DU (Old Street)
Discount Suit Company
29a Wentworth Street, E1 7TB (Aldgate East)
NOLA
68 Rivington Street, EC2A 3AY (Shoreditch High Street)
Casita
5a Ravey Street, EC2A 4QW (Old Street)

And on we could go, with a near-inexhaustible supply of kooky cocktail bars: **The Worship Street Whistling Shop** with its odd name and still odder drinking booth whose centrepiece is a tin bath; the **Discount Suit Company** hidden in a basement near Petticoat Market on precisely the last street in the capital you would expect to find a swanky bar; and **NOLA** a top-floor bar themed around the culture of New Orleans. One final recommendation for the area: **Casita**, a preposterously tiny Mexican bar. At the time of writing, it's surrounded by four separate building sites, and hidden along an anonymous sidestreet, making it one of those places you simply couldn't stumble across. I've never spotted a drinks menu yet, but you're better off asking the bar staff to recommend something.

Peg + Patriot
Patriot Square, E2 9NF (Bethnal Green or Cambridge Heath)

Further east brings you to the rapidly gentrifying Bethnal Green, and the supremely inventive spot that is Peg + Patriot. The bar is starkly furnished, letting the drinks (and the customers) do all the talking. Here you might find yourself sipping a teacake martini, or even a Marmite martini, while their ant-protein shakes (I'm told) are both nutritious and delicious. The intriguingly named Doncaster Miners Club Cocktail, meanwhile, contains genuine coal.

SOUTH

Hutong
The Shard, 31 Saint Thomas Street, SE1 9RY (London Bridge)

Most people heading to The Shard for a drink will end up in Aqua Shard. Hutong actually looks down on that bar from a floor or two up. The main area is given over to much-booked-out restaurant space. However, the bar is a delight, cocooned in dark-wood panelling. The cocktails are up to the standards you'd hope, and are as much of a draw as the epic views.

WEST

Egerton House Hotel
17–19 Egerton Terrace, SW3 2BX (South Kensington)

This hotel bar, at the western reaches of Knightsbridge, offers an intimate option that often evades the guidebooks. The head bartender Antonio has over 40 years experience, and is reckoned to serve up some of the best martinis in London. At £18 a glass, this might not be to everyone's budget, but then when was Knightsbridge ever to everyone's budget? This is a highly rated five-star hotel, with original works by Picasso, Matisse and Toulouse-Lautrec hanging on its walls.

AT THIS HOUR:

What event has taken place just before 10pm every night for at least 700 years? It's the Ceremony of the Keys, a peculiar little custom particular to the Tower of London. By applying online in advance, you can be there to watch servicemen and beefeaters perform their unique locking-up routine. "Halt! Who comes there?"; "The keys."; "Whose keys?"; "Queen Elizabeth's keys."... and so on. (I don't want to give away any spoilers... not least how they manage to eject the nightly group of onlookers *after* the gates have been so fervidly locked.)

10 pm
LATE-NIGHT FUN

The club scene seems to be in the doldrums right now, with many famous venues and nights winding up: the loss of the Astoria to Crossrail development was seen by many as a death knell. But people should have more faith in London. A city this inventive and protean will always evolve and find new ways forward. As with other areas, the trend seems to be for convergence, with clubs, restaurants and bars all merging into one experience. But you can still find plenty of places to party hard. Here's a small sample, chosen for variety.

CENTRAL

Dirty Martini
11–12 Russell Street, WC2B 5HZ (Covent Garden)

With live DJs and a magnetic attractiveness to party groups, these bars (others exist in Mayfair and the City) can really buzz at the weekends. The cocktails are pretty good for a chain, though they're a tiny bit more expensive than something like an All Bar One.

Fabric
77a Charterhouse Street, EC1M 6HJ (Farringdon)

Housed in an old cold store, Fabric remains one of the best-known and biggest clubs in the capital, some 15 years after it first opened. Three rooms, one of which is equipped with a vibrating floor, offer the best live DJ sets for anyone looking for a good old rave-style environment. You will get lost.

New Evaristo Club
57 Greek Street, W1D 3DX (Tottenham Court Road)

One of the best places to stay out late is, of course, Soho, with its mashed-together clientele of tourists, local workers and bona-fide Londoners. The area is now a shy approximation

of the seedy-cum-hedonistic quarter it once was, but you can still find plenty of interesting bars. The nearest you'll get to Old Soho is the tatty/cool New Evaristo Club, a basement bar that has so few pretensions that you'd probably get egged if you mentioned craft cocktails. Bottles of beer are the order of the night down here, the toilet is a joke, and the whole place looks like the model for a thousand gangster shows. But you have to pretend to love the New Evaristo Club – it's one of those unwritten London rules from which nobody may deviate.

Heaven
The Arches, Villiers Street, WC2N 6NG (Embankment)

Central London's biggest live venue, is atmospherically scrunched beneath the railway arches of Charing Cross station. The club dates back as far as 1979, and is a well-known linchpin of the LGBT community. Live sets from bands and DJs, the long-running Monday night Popcorn! party and rehomed nights from the now-closed Astoria add a breadth to the club that few other venues can muster.

NORTH

The Star of Kings
126 York Way, N1 0AX (King's Cross St Pancras)

Once upon a time, King's Cross was famous for its club scene. All that is long gone, swept away by gentrification and the huge developments behind the station, whose owners resolutely refuse a nightclub. Yet this old venue (formerly the Cross Kings) keeps something of the flame alive, with regular live music nights in the surprisingly roomy basement. It keeps on rocking through until 2am at weekends, and is a decent enough pub the rest of the time.

Proud Camden
The Stables Market, Chalk Farm Road, NW1 8AH (Chalk Farm)

Built into a former horse hospital, Proud does a little bit of everything and does it well. By day, it's a relatively laid-back bar and restaurant on the edge of Camden Market, with an art gallery thrown in for good measure. By night, it's famed for live music, cabaret and all-round partying… even stand-up comedy. It's like the Stephen Fry of nightclubs.

SOUTH

Adventure Bar
38 Clapham High Street, SW4 7UR (Clapham Common)

A cocktail involving edible insects? Well, this is called the Adventure Bar. Its branches here, in nearby Battersea and Covent Garden, offer a fun halfway house between bar and nightclub, staying open until 2am at weekends. The bars have a pricey but nicey range of cocktails, including vodkas infused with your favourite childhood sweets, such as flying saucers and Fox's Glacier Mints. The Clapham version throws in all kinds of playful touches, including menus distributed in old VHS cases (finally, someone has found a use for them).

Roller Disco
The Renaissance Rooms, Miles Street, SW8 1RZ (Vauxhall)

Vauxhall is, of course, full of highly rated night clubs. One of the more unusual puts its patrons on eight wheels: Roller Disco, catering for a mostly early 20s set, offers two skating rooms and a cheesy 70s/80s soundtrack so you can relive your childhood with the advantage of booze. Open till 2am at weekends.

EAST

All Star Lanes
95 Brick Lane, E1 6QL (Shoreditch High Street)

If you don't feel like dancing, how about a spot of ten-pin bowling? Big Lebowski fans can bowl away until 1am at weekends. All Star Lanes also offers a restaurant, bar and karaoke booths – kind of like a late-night leisure centre of fun. The Holborn sister-venue (Victoria House, Bloomsbury Place, WC1B 4DA) runs even later, kicking out at 2am.

Dalston Superstore
117 Kingsland High Street, E8 2PB (Dalston Kingsland)

Live DJs fuel one of east London's foremost party scenes from Wednesday until Sunday. Essentially a café-restaurant in the day, after 10pm the beats get louder and the long, thin space soon fills up with a mostly (but not exclusively) young LGBT crowd looking for dance and electronica.

WEST

Jam Tree
541 Kings Road, SW6 2EB (Fulham Broadway)

This laid-back late-nighter inhabits that fuzzy space between Chelsea and Fulham. The outside is unremarkable, drab even, but step inside and you're in a world of colour and polished metal. The wine list is epic, but it is to the roll call of cocktails to which you are hereby commended. Most involve some species of jam, with perhaps a dollop of Nutella or peanut butter. There's a sizeable garden at the back, a separate cocktail bar upstairs, and a sister venue in Clapham. Open until 2am at weekends, you'll never want to leave.

The Toy Shop
32 Putney High Street, SW15 1SQ (Putney)
Putney has long been served by excellent bars, pubs and restaurants for locals, but is increasingly getting a reputation as a destination in its own right. The Toy Shop bar leads the way, with a bustling, brightly coloured bar and restaurant that would look right at home in Covent Garden. Split on two levels, with both intimate booths and long banquettes, this place works well for small or large gatherings. It stays open until 2am at weekends, when a real party vibe kicks in.

11 pm
GETTING HOME

This hour is hard-wired into the brains of generations of British drinkers as the traditional serving of Last Orders before the pub closes for the night. Although this is still something of a default setting for many places, later licences are gradually sweeping across the city, and the 24-hour tube can only accelerate things. That said, it's likely that 11pm will remain the busiest night hour, as people cling to old habits and retreat back home. Here are a few tips for surviving the melée.

TUBES

Never sit down on the tube. You never know what variety of drunkard will embark at this time of night, and you wouldn't want to get trapped among a rowdy group of lagered-up football supporters. Standing also enables you to leap out of the way, should you find yourself next to a vomit-monger.

BUSES

If you happen to be a sociology student, the top deck of the night bus will swiftly provide you with a dozen ideas for a final-year thesis. The wretched hive of inebriated malcontents makes the Mos Eisley Cantina from Star Wars look like a Rotary Club. A general gradation of drunkenness can be detected on this upper deck. The front seats are taken by the merely tipsy – a good bet if you fancy a pleasant natter. The crowd gets more voluble towards the middle of the bus, where you'll find garrulous groups reliving the past few hours of drunken misadventure. Towards the back, we encounter the quiet ones: those who have tanked up so much booze that they're unlikely to wake up before Stockwell Bus Garage. Choose your seat according to your own insobriety or, better yet, remain downstairs.

BOATS

We all know about the night buses, and now the night tubes, but have you ever boarded the night boat? Thames Clippers run services from the London Eye to Woolwich as late as 11.13pm. It'll get you to Greenwich in a little over half an hour and, unlike the tube, it has a fully stocked bar.

BIKES

If you haven't been drinking, the cycle-hire scheme can be an effective way to get around at this time. Traffic levels tend to be lower and, if you stick to the back streets, you can have yourself a very pleasant nocturnal ride.

CABS

Finally, and seriously, never jump into a minicab that hasn't been pre-ordered. Black cabs are fully licenced and a safe option, but any other type of car that picks up without a booking is operating illegally. Avoid.

12 midnight

NIGHT THOUGHTS

Midnight: the Witching Hour. The city is handed over, from the people of the day to the creatures of the night. Outside the West End and a few satellite pockets, the metropolis quietens down.

London looks different. While the streets slumber, the skyline comes alive as indifferent skyscrapers blaze in glory. The upper floors of the Shard become a towering beacon, its distinctive summits sparkling like aureate tweezers. The jet black Tower 42 is bejewelled with lambent cinctures and a beryl crown. In the distance, the main Canary Wharf tower flashes like a latter-day lighthouse, alerting pilots heading into City Airport. The illuminated skyline is repeated in a shimmering Thames reflection.

London sounds different. Plane trees sussurate in the absence of engines. The chimes of Big Ben carry across the town – I've heard the bells from as far away as Hampstead Heath. No pigeons trouble the streets, and no gulls shriek overhead. The occasional reveller bellows on a nearby street. Vehicles, when they do appear, move with a speed not possible during the day. Or else they dawdle: council vehicles sucking up litter or washing down kerbs; night buses decelerating to a stop. The Thames itself can be heard, lapping against its embankments in the wake of a police launch or returning pleasure cruiser.

London smells different: the smog of the day lifts, drawing in fresher air. Around the West End, the whiff is of perfume, aftershave, vaporised alcohol and frying onions. The back streets around Chinatown stink of fermenting food waste, and all alleys broadcast a suspicion of urine. In the City, on a drizzly evening, you can smell the stones themselves.

To be out at night was once an offence. For many centuries, those found on the streets after dark were treated with suspicion, open to challenge. A walk through the night can still feel felonious. With so few rival distractions, your passing presence becomes the momentary highlight of every bored security guard. There is mutual suspicion between any two strangers who pass in the night. Why are you here? Why am I

AT THIS HOUR:

It's still possible to indulge in some culture during the Witching Hour. In the summer months, Shakespeare's Globe Theatre (21 New Globe Walk, SE1 9DT) puts on 'Midnight Matinees' of the Bard's plays. Load up with caffeine first, or you might find yourself nodding off to sleep (perchance to dream?) during the three-hour performances. All's well that ends well, however, with a warming breakfast in the neighbouring Swan restaurant for anyone who attends.

here? What business can anyone have on Lombard Street at four in the morning?

These anxieties exhilarate. We become uneasy with the familiar. A street walked 100 times by day can feel entirely new by night. Such are the attractions of night walking. Are you ready...?

1 am

A WALK THROUGH THE CITY

The metropolis is in recess. Most of the many millions are in bed. For night owls with no instinct for clubbing or for drinking, this is a sublime hour for exploring the City. And I use the word with the capital 'C'. The City of London, or the Square Mile, is among the most densely packed areas of town during the day, and long into the evening. Its medieval streets can barely contain the throng of office workers who must reach their desks, wine bars and sushi shops. In the early hours of the morning, everything is different. The silence can startle. These roads are the oldest in London, where remnants of the Roman city rub shoulders with the medieval, Georgian, Victorian and modern. An ancient church may parley with a skyscraper. In both senses of the superlative, the City holds the richest concentration of architecture in London. At night, it looks its best.

Start at **Chancery Lane tube station**; like many stations this is now open all night on Fridays and Saturdays. You are at the very western part of the Square Mile, as suggested by the two imposing dragon sculptures guarding the roadway. As we head east, High Holborn slopes downward slightly into the ancient valley of the River Fleet, long ago converted into a sewer. The valley becomes even more obvious once on **Holborn Viaduct**, a Victorian intervention to span the chasm. Ahead lie the silhouettes of St Sepulchre's Church and the *Lady Justice*-topped dome of the Old Bailey, on the site of the notorious Newgate Prison. These landmarks are in ancient concord. A handbell, still kept in the church, would be rung outside the condemned criminal's cell at midnight before an execution.

Head south, down the road known as Old Bailey, until you reach Ludgate Hill. In doing so, you follow the Roman and medieval city walls, whose remnants still linger beneath the buildings on your left. Glance up Ludgate to see the famous dome of **St Paul's**, gloriously illuminated yet recalling that dreadful night in 1940 when every street around the cathedral blazed with the firebombs of the Blitz. Cross, and duck down **Pageantmaster Court**. Here, the City is at its quietest, as we explore some of the capital's most ancient streets. Follow the road round to the left and on to **Carter Lane**. This ranks among the most atmospheric parts of the city, with a wide variety of architecture crowding in over the street. Shakespeare lived hereabouts, close to the site of the Cock Tavern. Exchanges and conversations overheard on these byways must have informed his writing.

Halfway down Carter Lane, look out for the unusual Venetian-style building on the left. This is surely London's most attractive youth hostel: hopefully, they're all asleep by this time. Directly opposite is the surreally named **Wardrobe Place**. It takes its name from the King's Wardrobe, the department of the Royal Household concerned with the monarch's clothing, which was formerly based here. Today, the cul-de-sac contains serviced apartments, which I'm told are cheaper to hire than hotel rooms in this area. Carter Lane soon opens out into St Paul's Churchyard, where the cathedral dominates the view. Few people know this, but that mighty dome is merely a bauble. The weight of the lantern structure on top is supported by two hidden inner-domes, while the familiar profile is just for show. Even less well known, the entire hemisphere was lifted up from the body of the cathedral by a bomb blast one night in 1940. It only moved upwards a fraction of an inch, but a hairline crack can still be seen (by those with privileged access) around the dome's perimeter.

As St Paul's Churchyard debouches into Cannon Street, look out for the imposing red-brick building on your right. This is

Bracken House, a post-war development notable for its arcane zodiacal clock, which features Winston Churchill's face as a centrepiece. It is, without question, one of the loopiest architectural features in London.

We're in the heart of the City now, and any road you care to follow would offer a layer cake of historical associations and anecdotes. Head, instead, for the merciless silhouette of **One New Change**, an angular glass shopping centre said to be inspired by the profile of a stealth ship. It doesn't work, even at night. The building is indisputably ugly and obtrudes on the cathedral like a slug devouring a macaron. Tiptoe past its southern flank, along **Watling Street**, a rare road alignment in the City that has existed since Roman times. Part of the way down, head north along **Bow Lane**, a remarkable network of closely drawn alleys that give a flavour of the medieval city that was destroyed in the Great Fire. Some are dead ends, others lead through – enjoy the exploration.

You should eventually emerge beneath **St Mary-le-Bow**, a Christopher Wren church that was largely demolished by the Blitz, but has since been seamlessly rebuilt. This houses the famous 'bow bells' from which traditional Cockneys are aurally judged. Its tintinnabulation can be heard today, and true Cockneys are born, still within earshot, at nearby St Bart's.

Cheapside derives its name from the Old English *chepe*, meaning market. This was the Oxford Street of medieval times. Subsidiary roads like Bread Street, Milk Street and Poultry hint further at this commercial past, partially restored (albeit in a way that would have boggled 13th-century shoppers) by the One New Change complex and other recent mixed-use developments.

Cheapside slopes gently down into the valley of the now-buried River Walbrook, where we reach the familiar junction of **Bank station**. The unholy trinity of politics, money and commerce are represented by Mansion House, the Bank of England and the Royal Exchange (itself now a luxury shopping and dining centre). This grand imperial statement offers a world-famous view of the capital to rival Piccadilly Circus, but just a road or two over and we can slip into another London. Work your way over the junction to **Lombard Street**, one of the few streets in the capital to have retained the ancient tradition of hanging street signs. Look out for the grasshopper sign. This is the sigil of Thomas Gresham, founder of the original Royal Exchange.

We're now approaching the greatest warren of alleyways in London. Duck into Change Alley – a favoured stopping point for tour guides who like to make stories up about the enigmatic name... it's another reference to the Royal Exchange. I'm not going to guide you through these passages – I'm not sure I could – but take your time wandering around looking at the various plaques and commemorations. You might even find another grasshopper or two, as well as the original London coffee house. Finish off beside **St Michael Cornhill**, noting its ornate Gothic doorway. The next alley along is St Peter's Alley. Look up, and if the moon is bright enough you should see one of the most menacing sights in the City: a trio of red she-devils peering down at passers-by. Legend has it that they were erected by the building's owners in retaliation against the church, which had obstructed development of the building. Whatever their origins, the devils prove that it always pays to look up when walking around the City.

On that spooky note, you're now just a five minute walk away from an all-night café in Liverpool Street. The next hour awaits...

2 am

OPEN ALL NIGHT

The first rule of very-late-night dining in London: kebabs are not your only option. At the time of writing, places that stay open until 1am are reasonably common, especially with many bars and pubs offering food. Later venues are more scarce, so I'm limiting this section to restaurants and cafés where you can still order food at 2am. Only a handful of 24-hour food outlets currently exist, mostly near stations and nightclubs. All that is likely to change with the arrival of all-night tube services, so this section is more a record of 'how things are' rather than how they will be in the near future.

CENTRAL

Bar Italia
22 Frith Street, W1D 4RF (Leicester Square)

The archetypal all-nighter, a place where you can grab an espresso at any hour, then negotiate your way down a frighteningly steep set of stairs to the toilet. The place was immortalised (if it wasn't already immortal) in the closing song on Pulp's 1995 album *Different Class*, 'There's only one place we can go, it's round the corner in Soho, where other broken people go...let's go.' As a bonus reason for going, the upstairs room was the place where TV was first publicly demonstrated by John Logie Baird in 1926. The café is open until 5am every day, then reopens at 7am for breakfast.

Old Compton Street
(Leicester Square)

Soho is far and away the best bet for finding late-night snacks. Old Compton Street mainstay **Café Boheme** has a night-owl menu served until 3am that includes French nibbles such as Croque Monsieur and Steak frites. The neighbouring **Soho Kitchen & Bar** matches that opening time, but offers a wider menu of light bites and mains leaning towards US cuisine. If 3am is too early, then a few doors down will bring you to

Balans Café, which has the full gamut of café classics and never seems to close. Meanwhile, nearby Chinatown offers a selection of nocturnal options, including **Mr Kong** (21 Lisle Street, WC2H 7BA, until 2.45am) **The Royal Dragon** (30 Gerard Street, W1D 6JS, until 3am) and **HK Diner** (22 Wardour Street, W1D 6QQ, until 4am).

Hippodrome Casino
Cranbourne Street, WC2H 7JH
(Leicester Square)

The Hippodrome never closes its doors and runs a 24-hour menu of sandwiches, burgers, salads and snacks. As casinos go, it's a very laid-back place, where half the punters are there for the bars and restaurants rather than to gamble. Plenty of history to mop up, and plenty of space, too.

VQ
111a Great Russell Street, WC1B 3NQ
(Tottenham Court Road)

Bloomsbury's VQ succinctly gives its opening times away in its name (at least if you're good at cryptic crosswords). VQ stands for Vingt-Quatre, which of course means '24' in French – perhaps they were going for something more sophisticated than the restaurant's previous name of Up All Night. Either way, this café-diner never closes. Contrary to the Gallic name, however, this is more an English/US affair, with everything from hot dogs to a fry-up on its impressively extensive menu. One senses that this mini-chain is well geared up to expand, now that the tubes are matching its opening hours.

Maroush
4 Vere Street, W1G 0DH (Bond Street)

For something east-Mediterranean that ranks above the typical kebab, check out the Maroush empire of eateries. The one on Vere Street serves up mezza and more until 5am (Thurs–Sat). Its parent branch on Edgware Road can only manage a paltry 2am, but the nearby Ranoush Juice, owned by the same group, keeps serving until 3am.

Tinseltown
44–46 St John Street, EC1M 4DF (Farringdon)

Farringdon clubbers are well catered for by US diner-style restaurant Tinseltown, which keeps on serving until 3am or 4am depending on the day. The subterranean den includes small tables and large banquette booths, to cater for any group size.

EAST

Beigel Bake
159 Brick Lane, E1 6SB (Shoreditch High Street)

This famous bakery can be considered the east London equivalent of Bar Italia. It serves very different food (obviously), but stands out as the 'rite of passage' all-nighter that every Londoner finds themselves in at some point. That's not to deny the quality on offer. For less than £2, you can have yourself a prize beigel and some new friends, met in the inevitable queue. It's worth splashing out a bit more for the salt beef beigel, for which this café is justly famous.

DALSTON HANGOUTS

Voodoo Ray's
95 Kingsland High Street, E8 2PB (Dalston Kingsland)
Sömine
131 Kingsland High Street, E8 2PB (Dalston Kingsland)
The Love Shake
5 Kingsland Road, E2 8AA (Hoxton)

Dalston has a few options for the nocturnally peckish. Pizza seekers can nibble on a doughy disc until 3am (Fri–Sat) at the much-vaunted **Voodoo Ray's**, above Dance Tunnel. This New York-style pizzeria serves by slice, a simple but crowd-pleasing idea that means you don't get stuck with just one recipe. Meanwhile, **Sömine** is a popular haunt with homeward-bound clubbers, offering all-night Turkish cuisine, including stews and soups that'll help you rehydrate. Heading back towards the centre of town, **The Love Shake** offers hotdogs and oddball milkshakes until 2.30am (occasionally 4.30am on Saturdays).

Polo Bar
176 Bishopsgate, EC2M 4NQ (Liverpool Street)

The relatively stylish (well, it's got white tiles everywhere) Polo Bar will serve you a superior fry-up or burger at any hour of the day or night. It's right opposite Liverpool Street Station and so sports a mixed clientele of Shoreditch clubbers and eighth-cup-of-the-nighters who missed their last train home.

Duck & Waffle
110 Bishopsgate, EC2N 4AY (Liverpool Street)

If you're looking for something a bit more sophisticated, the Heron Tower's Duck and Waffle restaurant serves throughout the night, offering expensive but excellent repasts (including some duck with some waffle). You're at the highest publicly accessible point in the Square Mile here (only The Shard across the river tops it), and the views are unsurprisingly magnificent. Plus, you get to ride the scariest lifts in London, which cling to the outside of the building and fly up with dizzying speed.

WEST

Maroush
38 Beauchamp Place, SW3 1NU (Knightsbridge)
Ranoush
86 High Street Kensington, W8 4SG (High Street Kensington)
VQ
325 Fulham Road, SW10 9QL (Fulham Broadway)
Yas
7 Hammersmith Road, W14 8XJ (Kensington Olympia)

Away from the bright lights of the West End and the nightclubs of the east, late night dining is something of a scarcity. A second branch of Lebanese restaurant **Maroush** in Knightsbridge stays open until 5am, and claims to pull in the celebrities. Sister restaurant **Ranoush** on High Street Kensington will serve you till 3am. Likewise, a second non-stop branch of **VQ** (see page 119) can be found on Fulham Road. As with its Bloomsbury twin, it never closes. Fans of Persian cuisine could try **Yas** on the Hammersmith Road. It gets mixed reviews – mainly concerning the service rather than the quality of the food – but keeps on cooking until 4am.

NORTH

Green Lanes
(Manor House or Turnpike Lane)

Tinseltown
104 Heath Street, NW3 1DR (Hampstead)

Since Camden Town's legendary Marathon Kebab lost its late licence, the north is somewhat lacking in iconic late-nighters. Your best bet might be a jaunt along Green Lanes, where the lengthy parade of Turkish restaurants includes several open into the early hours. And then Hampstead (of all places) has a branch of Tinseltown open until 3am at weekends (2am otherwise), serving up diner-style treats.

SOUTH

Bagel King
280 Walworth Road, SE17 2TE (Elephant and Castle)
Golden Grill
20 Camberwell Green, SE5 7AA (Denmark Hill)
Blackheath Tea Hut
Goffers Road, SE3 0UA (Lewisham)

South London is also spartanly furnished with late-night eating options. **Bagel King** on Walworth Road might not look particularly regal, but it's a much appreciated 24-hour stop-off point for Jamaican food and, of course, bagels. For something a bit meatier, the **Golden Grill** in Camberwell lasts until 4am, with an endless menu of pizzas, kebabs, burgers and other fast food options. You probably don't have any respectable business being out on Blackheath at four in the morning, but if you do, the legendary **Blackheath Tea Hut** should see you right with a cuppa and something warm to eat, like a burger or a bacon roll. It's open 24 hours.

3 am

GHOSTLY LONDON

You might be still awake, but by 3am the mind plays tricks. Most ghost sightings occur in the quiet hours, when witnesses are conscious yet still oneiric. This is the hour for another nocturnal sojourn, in search of the capital's many phantoms. London's two most famous 'haunted houses' – the Tower of London and Hampton Court Palace – are sadly off limits at this hour, but you'll find plenty of creepy corners around the city. I have to confess, I'm no believer in spirits, but even the most rational or sceptical person can be entertained by a good ghost story.

CENTRAL

London's Most Haunted
50 Berkeley Square, W1J 5BA (Bond Street)

One of the capital's most notorious haunted houses can be found in this leafy Mayfair square. The imposing townhouse at number 50 was once owned by Prime Minister George Canning and has long served as Maggs Bros book shop. It's more famous for its ghost, however, which is said to haunt the upper floors. The story seems to change with each retelling, but normally involves some hideous wraith scaring the occupants to death or suicide. I would be happy to spend a night alone there, if the owners would care to let me in.

Haunted trees
Green Park (Green Park)

The Royal Park is accessible at all hours of day or night. Many writers have described the space as melancholic or subdued. Lepers were buried here in medieval times, and a 17th-century plague pit has been found in the northern section. No wonder that the park has attracted some of the capital's most chilling supernatural associations. The grounds are said to contain a 'death tree', which moans and chuckles at those who would seek its shelter. Another arbour is home to a ghastly pig-faced creature whose appearance is rancid enough to scare a person to death. Other visitations include a hanging man, a cut-throat suicide and even a troupe of pixies. This park really is spook central.

Black dog
Amen Court, EC4M 7BU (St Paul's)

Perhaps the spookiest location you can possibly visit at 3am is Amen Court in the City of London. This tight cul-de-sac backs onto the Old Bailey, and includes a section of masonry from the infamous Newgate Jail. A foul-smelling black shape – sometimes a dog, possibly an inebriated banker – has supposedly been seen slithering along the wall. Some say the ghostly form is the shade of a medieval mystic, slain by the starving prison inmates, who subsequently ate him. In revenge, he returned as a phantom hound, eternally bent on sniffing out his tormentors. If you make the nocturnal visit, be aware that you'll be snooping around behind the Old Bailey in the dead of night – the imposing suit of a curious security guard might be the most menacing black shape to materialise in front of you.

NORTH

Phantom bantam
Pond Square, N6 6BA (Highgate)

Still more peculiar is the spectral chicken of Highgate (I'm not making this up). The phantom bantam pecks around Pond Square. Legend has it that philosopher Sir Francis Bacon met his end after experimenting with frozen chicken and catching a fatal chill. For some reason, it's chicken not Bacon that haunts the square.

WEST

Ghost bus
Cambridge Gardens, W10 (Ladbroke Grove)

Ladbroke Grove claims London's most peculiar ghost: not a person, nor even an animal, but a phantom double-decker bus. The vehicular visitation haunts the corner of Cambridge Gardens and St Mark's Road. Witnesses describe an eerie number 7, all lights blaring but nobody on board, which would cause motorists to swerve. The bus would then vanish as mysteriously as it appeared.

Spooky squirrel
Brompton Cemetery, Fulham Road, SW10 9UG (Fulham Broadway)

Peer through the bars of Brompton Cemetery and see if you can spy the phantom red squirrel that supposedly scrabbles through the undergrowth here. Red squirrels have been absent from London for many decades, so he must have been dead for some time. The cheeky nutkin is said to be fond of thievery, stealing scarves, handkerchiefs and food from unwary passers-by.

GHOST STATIONS

Now that the tube is open 24 hours, will its spectral complement of ghosts be sighted more often? The hypogeal stations and tunnels have long excited the imaginations of the credulous. Platforms can be dimly lit, and prone to sudden draughts and strange rumbles – it is little wonder that the network has conjured so many eerie tales that the subject has spawned books and TV programmes.

Covent Garden tube is said to be the haunt of William Terriss, a famous Victorian stage actor stabbed to death near the tube station (a plaque marks the site on Maiden Lane). At Aldgate, a worker who received a 20,000-volt electric shock was apparently brought back to life by a mysterious vanishing lady, who was seen stroking the prone man's hair. Staff at Elephant and Castle are regularly disturbed by strange noises. Perhaps most eerily of all, drivers negotiating the Kennington Loop – a stretch of turnaround track not used by the public – often hear voices and bangings in the carriages behind their cab, even though all passengers should have alighted.

GHOST HUNTS

Finally, keep an eye out for overnight ghost hunts. These events are organised by a number of groups, with no particular regularity and with changing venues. They give you the opportunity to stay up all night in an historic building with a bunch of strangers, attempting to contact the dead. I once joined in a session at the Ragged School Museum. Despite the best asseverations of the mediums and mystics present, we just couldn't detect the legion of ghosts supposedly swirling around the room. In fact, the scariest moment was walking home through Mile End Park at 5am. Still, even for a non-believer the escapade was immense fun, and a chance to explore a landmark building in a unique way.

4 am

NIGHT MARKETS

While central London remains sleepy at 4am, some points of town are at their busiest. These are the main markets: they specialise in wholesale trade to restaurants and other outlets, but individuals can also walk in and grab a bargain.

Smithfield Market
East Market Building, EC1A 9PQ (Farringdon)

This is the most central, just around the corner from Farringdon station. Meat has been important to this location since medieval times, first as a livestock market and then, from Victorian times, as a place to buy butchered meat. Its existence in central London is threatened – the early morning rumble of lorries just isn't commensurate with the gentrified streets of Clerkenwell. But for now, visitors can enjoy the unique charm of the 19th-century buildings. Inside the market, meat is sold from individual counters much like any butchers. You'll find the prices much lower and open to haggling. Countless carcasses hang from rails. Ebullient porters and traders move around in blood-stained white overalls. An offal counter sports ox-feet, cheeks, pluck, trotters and something called black straps. This is not a place for vegetarians. Other counters offer exotic meats from overseas, pre-packaged for individual purchase. Be sure to take a peek inside the western-most hall, the poultry market. While most of the complex is preposterously Victorian in its architecture, this great hall was built in the 1950s. Its almost impossible roof could only be made from concrete, and sweeps over the space in what is known as a hyperbolic paraboloid. Try saying that at 4am. If you're still here come 7am, nearby The **Fox and Anchor** pub (115 Charterhouse Street, EC1M 6AA) opens early for market

breakfasts and/or a guilty pint. I can also recommend the nearby **La Forchetta** café (92 Cowcross Street, EC1M 6BH) for the best-value Full English breakfast I've ever had.

Billingsgate Fish Market
Trafalgar Way, E14 5ST (Blackwall)

This market traded from time immemorial at the area still known as Billingsgate within the Square Mile. Sadly, the whole lot was shifted out to a 13-acre (5.3ha) site in the Docklands in 1982. Here it remains, slightly incongruous next to the gleaming towers of Canary Wharf and its remarkable new Crossrail station. Changes are afoot, however. The market's future faces uncertainty, with plummeting fish stocks and increasing local land values. Visit while you can. You'll find countless species, many unfamiliar, from over 100 countries and including various types of shellfish. The freshest North Sea fish is snapped up by commercial customers early, but you should still find plenty at the counters from 4am.

New Covent Garden Market
SW8 (Vauxhall)

This is the UK's largest market for vegetables, fruit and flowers. Originally located in Covent Garden itself, the market now trades out in Nine Elms, beside one of the biggest redevelopment sites in the country. Forty per cent of all vegetables you eat in the restaurants of London come from here. Like the other markets, it's geared up for wholesalers, restaurateurs and other customers in need of large quantities. However, if you're after a complete refit for your flower beds, or are catering for a large group, you might consider wandering in. It's free if you turn up on foot, or £5 if you want to park. **New Spitalfields Market** in Leyton is the other big vegetable and fruit market, but almost entirely wholesale. If you're seeking a crate of exotic fruit or veg, however, it's perhaps the best source in London.

AT THIS HOUR:

Although much of the tube network now runs all night over the weekend, the trains still go to sleep for a few hours on Sunday through Thursday for engineering and maintenance. At the time of writing, the earliest possible train you can catch is the 04.38 Hammersmith and City line train from Hammersmith to Aldgate.

5 am

UP WITH THE SUN

Like the crackle of a campfire or the patter of rain when safely sheltered, witnessing the reappearance of the sun prompts an atavistic joy in most people. It is as though we are still vulnerable hunter-gatherers on the ancient planes, thankful to have survived the dangers of the darkness. Or perhaps it's just the smug feeling of being up and active while our fellow citizens slumber on. Who knows? In any case, London can be a magical place to watch the rising sun. All you need to do is look up the hour, then find a place with a relatively clear view to the east.

You needn't be a virtuous early bird to watch this quotidian marvel. Sunrise in London can be as late as 8.06am in December and January. On the other hand, you'll need to be in place as early as 4.43am to catch it around the Summer Solstice in June. Although this section is nominally set at 5am, the following ideas relate to the time of sunrise rather than that specific hour.

The classic option is to ascend Primrose Hill, the highest natural point close to central London. The park opens at 5am all year round, so you can be upon the summit for dawn at any time other than high summer.

Central London is more problematic, with so many buildings cluttering the horizon. Your best bet is to choose one of the bridges along the Thames. Decent eastward views can be gained from Waterloo, Blackfriars, Millennium and London Bridges. The latter must surely be the pick of the bunch, as it offers golden silhouette views of Tower Bridge.

The highest sunrise vantage point of all, and perhaps most expensive, is the 24-hour **Duck & Waffle** restaurant in the Heron Tower (see page 121). You may need to prebook, especially if you want to request an east-facing window. I once turned up at 5.30am on a Sunday to find the place almost full.

I've lied. Twice. There's another option at both greater altitude and greater cost. A dawn balloon flight over London is utterly magical and serene. **Adventure Balloons** offers morning flights from April to August on weekdays. They last about an hour and cost £200. This is by far the most memorable way to watch a London dawn, but it comes with its own frustrations (and not just the cost). Balloons are temperamental things and flights are often cancelled on the day because of unfavourable weather conditions.

Other activities suggest themselves at this auroral hour. Sun-up is associated with birdsong – the dawn chorus – one of the few overt natural phenomena to permeate the city, as it does the countryside. You can hear it anywhere, but large open spaces like the banks of the Thames or Blackheath might offer a particularly melodious experience.

Of course, being out when everybody else is asleep also presents a unique opportunity for photography. Much fun can be had walking around the normally bustling West End tourist sites and snapping them when devoid of people. One company, **Cities At Dawn** (www.citiesatdawn.com) even offers professional workshops on how to take the best photographs in the early morning light. Meeting times range between 4am and 6am depending on the time of year.

AT THIS HOUR:

One of London's ghost trains departs central London at 05.31. The service between Liverpool Street and Enfield Town operates just one train per week (Saturdays), with no return service. The irregularity means the train often leaves without a single passenger, so you can consider the driver your personal chauffeur. This, and several other services in London, are known as Parliamentary trains – routes that continue minimal operations to avoid the costs of formal closure. Other examples include the daily 11.36 Paddington to West Ruislip service, and the 06.18 from Battersea Park to Highbury and Islington.

THE LONDON
Year

Having compiled so many activities for specific hours of the day, it seems fitting to finish this book with a selection of London events specific to a particular day. This list could run for pages and pages if I were to list every annual festival. With a couple of exceptions, I focus on some of the smaller, lesser-known events, picking one for each month. I will happily buy you a drink if you manage to tick off all 12.

JANUARY

Commemoration of Charles I: The sight of civilians marching through Whitehall armed with guns and pikestaff might be the nightmare of every politician, but such a scene occurs every January in commemoration of Charles I. Hundreds of enthusiasts from the English Civil War Society assemble on the Mall to follow in the footsteps of their luckless hero, who was beheaded on 30 January 1649. Wreaths are laid at the Charles I statue and the site of his decollation at Mansion House. The procession is not well publicised and is usually witnessed only accidentally. It deserves a bigger audience.

FEBRUARY

Trial of the Pyx: This annual judicial ceremony sounds, and looks, like something from a *Harry Potter* novel. In early February, members of the judiciary assemble in Goldsmith's Hall to check the weight and quality of newly minted coins. Today, with machine-made cash, the procedure is effectively ceremonial, but it is still conducted by the Queen's Remembrancer with solemnity and seriousness. Several thousand coins must be tested, to achieve a representative sample of the number minted, but the assembled dignitaries only handle a fraction of the task. Public tickets to watch the ceremony are available each year, and it's worth getting hold of them if only to see inside the opulent livery hall in which the trial takes place.

MARCH

Oranges and Lemons Service: The church of St Clement Danes not only says 'oranges and lemons' in its bell toll, it also hands them out. On the third Thursday in March, at 1pm, the church conducts its annual Oranges and Lemons Service, following which a barrowful of citrus fruits is donated to local school children. Thankfully, the nursery rhyme is not played out to its conclusion, and nobody loses their head.

APRIL

The Widow's Buns: The biggest attraction of the Widow's Son pub in Bromley-by-Bow is its out-of-date food. Some of its hot cross buns were baked decades ago, and are black with age (and a fire that consumed some of them in the 1980s). It's a tradition, stretching back to early Victorian times, to hang a fresh bun from the ceiling every Good Friday. Legend has it that the mother of a sailor would bake an Easter bun for her boy every year in the hope that he would return from sea. He never did, and she carried on accumulating buns until her death. A pub was built on the site and carried on the tradition it maintains to this day (I've seen a press report from 1898, when there were already 60 ageing baps on the premises). Pop along on Good Friday and watch a sailor from the Royal Navy add to the mouldy stockpile.

MAY

Miglia Quadrato: London's very own version of the Wacky Races takes place in the City of London in mid-May. This motoring treasure hunt runs between midnight and 5am, which means few people other than the City of London Police have heard about it. Competitors have five hours to solve 60 clues, each of which leads to a specific location within the Square Mile. Teams of up to six people can take part, with only one driver needed per team. While most people tackle the challenge in a modern car, plenty of ancient vehicles, including a just-about-roadworthy vintage fire engine race around the streets putting the willies up security guards. It's been organised by the United Hospitals and University of London Motoring Club for the past 55 years, and anyone can take part.

JUNE

Knollys Rose Rent: Every year, the Lord Mayor of London is sent a single rose from a garden on Seething Lane. The custom dates back to the 14th century. Tradition has it that while soldier Sir Robert Knollys was off fighting abroad, his wife built a footbridge over the lane to her rose garden, but failed to seek permission from City authorities. Rather than punish the hero's wife, the Lord Mayor instead asked only for a flower from the lady by way of a peppercorn rent. Six hundred and fifty years later, the floral tariff is still conveyed to the Lord Mayor's residence at Mansion House by a party representing the Company of Watermen and Lightermen. You can watch their short parade anywhere between Seething Lane and Bank, on a date in June that varies each year.

JULY

Swan Upping: Since the 12th century, the Crown has claimed ownership of all mute swans on open water – mostly because they taste very pleasant and make a conspicuous centrepiece on the banqueting table. In more recent centuries, ownership has been shared with two livery companies: the Vintners and the Dyers. Each year, skiffs representing the three parties travel up river on the lookout for swans. The birds are briefly captured, ringed, and put back into the water – but never eaten. Today, the practice is useful as well as ceremonial, as it provides information on the health of the bird population and the river in general. You can view the ceremony along the Thames at the western extremity of London and beyond in the third week of July.

AUGUST

Notting Hill Carnival: London tends to go quiet in August as many of us flock overseas and hand the city over to visitors. The striking exception is the Notting Hill Carnival, which shouts and sings and struts its way through the Bank Holiday weekend. The mood on the streets of W11 is so infectious that there are a million participants and no spectators. I include it among these lesser-known events because the big one is coming up. In 2016, the festival will celebrate its 50th birthday and is sure to be bigger and brasher than ever.

SEPTEMBER

The *Autumnal Equinox*. The point where daylight and darkness are evenly balance is marked each year by The Druid Order with a ceremony on Primrose Hill. Companions of the order dress in white robes and process to the hill's summit, where they form a circle and conduct a public ceremony. The time varies each year, but always takes place on 22, 23 or 24 September. A similar ceremony at Tower Hill marks the Spring Equinox. Simply turn up at the appropriate time to watch for free.

OCTOBER

Quit Rents: The Queen's Remembrancer, whom we last met in February's Trial of the Pyx, presides over more oddness in October, when he or she officiates at the Quit Rents ceremony at the Royal Courts of Justice. Here, the City pays the crown its annual rent for two properties – one in Shropshire, one in Westminster. Rather than paying cash, as you or I might, the City must cough up two knives (one blunt, one sharp), six horseshoes and 61 nails. As if that wasn't bizarre enough, the Crown then lends these items back to the City, so it can pay them again next year. Public tickets are usually made available to watch this choice spectacle.

NOVEMBER

Lord Mayor's Show: One of the better-known events in this collection takes place on the second Saturday in November. It commemorates the inauguration of the new Lord Mayor, and grew up centuries ago around that dignitary's mandatory procession to the monarch's representatives in Westminster. You can watch the pomp and ceremony on TV, but you really should get yourself along to the streets of the City to witness this colourful parade, which includes representatives from livery companies, military regiments and companies, schools and charities associated with the Square Mile. The highlight is the Lord Mayor's coach, an uncomfortable (I'm told!) gilded vehicle from the mid-18th century. My favoured spot is just outside the Guildhall on Gresham Street, whence you can witness the very start of the parade. Just be sure to get there an hour before the start to bag a place – there's a handy coffee shop next door.

DECEMBER

The Great Christmas Pudding Race: At a mere 35 years old, this is a relative newcomer as traditions go, but among the jolliest. Contestants dressed in gaudy seasonal costumes career around Covent Garden market, bouncing over inflatables while trying not to drop the Christmas puddings from their trays. The event raises thousands for Cancer Research UK, while putting a broad smile on the face of anyone who attends or takes part. A fine note to end upon.

ACKNOWLEDGEMENTS

Several people were very helpful in focusing my ideas for this book. I'd like to thank my fellow Londonist contributors Tabish Khan, Janan Jedrzejewski and Ben Norum for particularly useful discussions. I'd also like to thank the staff at Batsford for making this book happen. My wife Heather deserves unlimited credit for putting up with my excessive Londonophilia. Finally, I'd like to thank Thameslink trains for providing a new and unexpected adventure every day.

ABOUT THE AUTHOR

Matt Brown has spent more than a decade professionally exploring and writing about London. As the long-term editor of Londonist.com (now editor-at-large), he's waded through sewers, slept in a plague pit, climbed up behind the lights of Piccadilly Circus and canoed into catacombs in search of the capital's stories. His golden rule is to enter at least one building he's never been in before, every single day.

Matt is happy to be contacted about any London curiosities or anecdotes via i.am.mattbrown@gmail.com, or @mattfromlondon.

INDEX

MY BEST BOOZERS

MY QUIET PLACES

BEST PLACES TO EAT

MOST MEMORABLE MUSEUMS

WHERE TO TAKE MY FRIENDS

RETAIL THERAPY

GLORIOUS GALLERIES

BREATHTAKING BUILDINGS

WALKS WORTH MY TIME

THE BIG SMOKE'S BEAUTY SPOTS

UNFORGETTABLE TIPS